YORKSHIRE F
A Canoeist's Guide

British Canoe Union
Yorkshire and Humberside Region
Access and Recreation Committees

A Second Edition Prepared by
MIKE TWIGGS AND DAVID TAYLOR

Published by CORDEE Leicester

© British Canoe Union (Yorkshire Region) 1992

British Library Cataloguing-in-Publication Data
A catalogue record for this book is available from the British Library

ISBN 1 871890 16 0

This guidebook is available from all specialist equipment shops, and the book trade. It can also be obtained direct from the publishers, together with most other books for canoeists.

CORDEE
3a De montfort Street
Leicester
LE1 7HD

Front cover photo: The River Tees – between High Force and Low Force. Photo. by Alan Fox
Rear cover photo: The River Ure – open boat canoeing between Masham and Sleningford Watermill. Photo. by Sam Cook

Printed by Joseph Ward Colourprint Ltd
The Ring Road   Dewsbury   West Yorkshire

Contents

Acknowledgements

The British Canoe Union, Yorkshire and Humberside region wishes to thank the following people for contributions without which the 'Canoeist's Guide to Yorkshire Rivers' could not have been produced:

MIKE TWIGGS — for his organisation of the whole project and editing the text.

DAVID TAYLOR — for producing the maps in computerised form and for creating additional text.

MARIANNE SPENDER — for general help and guidance.

PAMELA AND NORMAN TAYLOR — for help with creating and editing the text.

MIKE MOXON — for providing the grid references.

THE LOCAL ACCESS OFFICERS — for updating the information in the guide and where necessary preparing new itineraries.

ALPHA PRINTING SERVICES LEEDS — for help in the initial production of the maps.

CORDEE PUBLISHERS — for their expert help in producing the guide in its final form.

Introduction

- by the Regional Access and Touring Recreation Officers

When the first Yorkshire and Humberside guide was published it was very well received by all canoeists who purchased it. But nothing stands still, and it soon became apparent that when the time came for a reprint, we would not only correct those mistakes and omissions which had been made in the first guide, but would also increase the number of rivers covered. I would like to thank all the Local Access Officers who have spent many hours in revising their sections of the guide but, please remember, no guide is perfect. Rivers are living things, they are altering all the time, some changes are man made or are caused by flood and happen very quickly.

It is essential to note that most white water rivers are private and where agreements have been negotiated the dates and times that the stretch of river is open for canoeing etc MUST be strictly adhered to, otherwise the future of the agreements is endangered. This requires that the Regional Access Officer, Local Access Officer or Regional Recreational Officer is contacted well in advance of any proposed use of such stretches if the paddler is in any way unsure of the terms of any agreement.

All readers, particularly those who have recently paddled the rivers described, are asked to send any experiences, suggestions, additions or corrections to:

Mike Twiggs
Regional Access Officer
38 Badger Gate
Threshfield
SKIPTON BD23 5EN
(Tel 0756 753101)

Colin Stegeman
Regional Recreation Officer
17 Quarry Road
RICHMOND DL10 4BP
(Tel 0748 823861)

The Central Council of Physical Recreation Water Sports Code

1. Avoid damage to banks and shoreline vegetation.
2. Avoid using areas important for wintering wildfowl, nesting birds and spawning fish in the appropriate season.
3. Whenever possible, come ashore from boats only at recognised landing places.
4. Do not trespass on private banks or moorings.
5. Do everything possible to avoid pollution. Do not throw litter or rubbish into the water or leave it lying about the banks.
6. Obey the general rules of navigation and any local bye-laws, but remember that, even when you have the right of way, you have an overriding responsibility to avoid collision.
7. Avoid crossing the bows of oncoming craft at close quarters.
8. Give precedence to others when they are engaged in organised competition.
9. Have special regard for the problems of the inexpert or beginner as you have for the learner driver on the road.
10. A hail is often useful to draw a person's attention to a situation which may result in inconvenience, damage to gear, or a collision; but treat a hail as a friendly warning and not as an insult.
11. Know the signs for the marking of areas used by underwater swimmers and divers.
12. In shallow water keep well clear of wading fishermen and leave adequate room both in front of and behind him for his cast. Keep well clear when he is playing a fish.
13. Make sure that your craft is safe and that sufficient safety equipment is carried at all times.
14. It is advisable to be in possession at all times of a Public Liability Insurance Policy (this is included in BCU membership).
15. All Governing bodies of watersports (including the BCU) produce extensive rules for safety and other matters. These should be read and understood before participating in any activity.
16. Keep away from banks from which anglers are fishing.
17. Keep well clear of anglers tackle, do not loiter in fishing pools, cause as little disturbance as possible.
18. Keep a sharp look out for fishermen. Comply with any signals they may make to indicate whether they wish you to wait for a moment or to pass. Give a hail if you think your approach has been unnoticed.
19. Be particularly careful not to touch anglers lines.
20. Do not alter course so as to baulk other craft, particularly in narrow waters. Remember that larger boats are less easily manoeuvrable and that canoes can use much shallower water than other craft.
21. Keep clear of rowing craft - sculls, fours and eights - particularly when racing or serious coaching is taking place. Remember that it is sometimes difficult for rowing craft to see canoes.

AND FINALLY

22. Do get the most from canoeing by being a member of the British Canoe Union.

The British Canoe Union

The British Canoe Union is canoeing's national organisation; formed in 1936, it now has over 700 affiliated clubs. The aim of the organisation is to unite everyone interested in the sport by providing a complete service to paddlers – improving access to rivers and canals, keeping members informed and encouraging the teaching of paddlers at all abilities, through the coaching scheme.

The British Canoe Union (BCU) is affiliated to the International Canoe Federation and the Olympic Association and is responsible for both national and international competitions.

BCU membership provides comprehensive insurance covering life, accident, equipment and third party liability, free canal and river licences, information and free advice, coaching of canoeing skills at special courses, proficiency tests and a regular colour magazine- 'Canoe Focus'. The Members' Year Book contains a host of information on activities, club details etc. In addition the BCU Canoeing Handbook and many specialist publications are available from the BCU to aid the individual paddler.

In order to get the most from canoeing it is recommended that you become a Member of the British Canoe Union. For all enquiries please contact:

> The British Canoe Union
> John Dudderidge House
> Adbolton Lane
> West Bridgford
> NOTTINGHAM NG2 5AS
> (Tel 0602 821100)

YORKSHIRE'S RIVERS

General Information

Public Rights of Passage by Boats

In England and Wales a sharp distinction is drawn by the law between the sea and tidal waters on the one hand and non-tidal waters on the other.

On the sea, and tidal waters up to the limit of high water mark at ordinary spring tides, the land covered by water is regarded as belonging to the Crown, which permits public navigation, as far as physical conditions allow.

Statutory and Common Law Navigations may be canoed at any time subject to Local Regulations, which may require you to have a licence or pay a fee. Additional information is given in the section entitled Navigations and Canals.

The public right to navigate is a right of passage only (either upstream or downstream). It does not entitle canoeists to 'occupy' a stretch of water for a canoeing event, practice or instruction. It does not entitle you to launch or land without the landowners permission, except at a public landing.

Private Rivers

It will be seen from the above that a certain amount of flat water is available as public navigation, but very little fast moving water falls into this category or is covered by access agreements. Although there are stretches of water where the riparian owners have not formally objected to canoeing taking place, the fact remains that most white water rivers are private. Where agreements have been negotiated it is absolutely essential that dates and times during which a stretch of river is open for canoeing etc are strictly adhered to otherwise the future of the agreements is endangered. This requires that the Regional Access Officer, Local Access Officer or Touring Officer is contacted well in advance of any proposed use of such stretches if the paddler is in any way unsure of the terms of an agreement.

Canoeing and the Environment

Environmental issues have come to assume great importance in recent years in relation to all types of waterways. The interface between canoeing as a sport and the water environment in which it is conducted has great potential value. Canoeing offers unrivalled opportunities to explore and observe the wildlife and landscape associated with our rivers, while being itself an inherently 'green' activity. It causes no erosion, noise or pollution and does not alter or damage the environment in any way PROVIDED THAT CANOEISTS OBSERVE THE CCPR CODE OF CONDUCT outlined elsewhere in this guide.

The detrimental effects of water pollution derive from many sources including inadequate sewage disposal systems, excessive use of nitrogenous fertilizers, and dumping of industrial waste. Canoeists, particularly those who paddle an area regularly, are well placed to detect adverse changes in the environment and inform the relevant bodies where necessary, such as the National Rivers

Authority. The Environmental Conservation Panel of the BCU is responsible for monitoring environmental issues in relation to canoeing. In addition, the BCU Regional Officers take part in local Riverwatches which have been set up in several areas by diverse associations and groups of people with the common aim of improving the quality of our waterways.

Further information may be obtained from the BCU Yorkshire and Humberside Region Environmental Officer:

Norman Taylor
73 Gateland Lane
Shadwell
LEEDS LS17 8LN
(Tel 0532 737393)

National Rivers Authority

The National Rivers Authority (NRA) was set up in order to monitor river pollution and improve the quality of our waterways; to plan water resources; to carry out flood defence work and promote conservation of the water environment and protect its amenity. There is a 24 hour emergency reporting line at regional headquarters for notification of environmental problems on waterways:

National Rivers Authority
Yorkshire Region
Rivers House
21 Park Square South
LEEDS LS1 2QG
(Tel 0532 440191)

Fishing Seasons

Some agreements on access are tied to the fishing seasons which for the rivers in the Yorkshire Region are as follows:

Coarse Fishing Close Season   14 March to 16 June.
Trout Fishing Close Season   1 October to 24 March inclusive.

The canal navigations are exempt from the above with certain exceptions. The NRA will on request supply details of these.

River Grading

I.   EASY. Occasional small rapids, waves regular and low. Correct course easy to find, but care is needed with obstacles like pebble banks, protective works, fallen trees etc., especially on narrow rivers.

II.   MEDIUM. Fairly frequent rapids, usually with regular waves, easy eddies, or whirlpools. Course generally easy to recognise.

III.   DIFFICULT. Numerous rapids with fairly high irregular waves, broken water, eddies and whirlpools. Course not always easily recognisable.

IV.   VERY DIFFICULT. Long and extended stretches of rapids with high irregular waves, difficult broken water, eddies and whirlpools. Course often difficult to recognise. Inspection from the bank nearly always necessary.

V.   EXCEEDINGLY DIFFICULT. Long unbroken stretches of rapids with difficult and completely irregular broken water, submerged rocks, very difficult whirlpools and very fast eddies. Previous inspection absolutely essential.

VI.   THE ABSOLUTE LIMIT OF DIFFICULTY. All previously mentioned difficulties increased to the limit of practicability, cannot be attempted without risk to life.

A rise or fall in water level always alters a river's appearance and the grading of the stretch in question, and may make it easier or quite impracticable in difficulty. The gradings given are, as far as possible, for favourable water conditions.

Rough water trips should not be undertaken unless the canoeist can swim well, has a craft in sound order, and good technique and boat control. There should always be at least 2 other boats. Newcomers to rough water rivers should not attempt anything beyond grade III and there should be an experienced leader and an appropriate number of canoeists. Grade IV is a real testing, even for experienced canoeists. Grades V and VI should not be touched except by the most experienced white water canoeists. Itineraries and maps can only give very general directions, and there may be a real danger of loss of life. Weirs present many special problems and if deemed shootable should still only be descended after inspection and under safe conditions.

Canoeists with Special Needs

The Region actively encourages canoeing activities for people with disabilities or special needs. Anyone needing advice or wishing to organise a canoeing activity of any sort involving people with special needs should contact:

> John Swallow
> The Mistle
> Scotland Lane
> Horsforth
> LEEDS LS18 5HP
> (Tel 0532 589415)

Regional Information Line

A telephone line with a 24 hour answerphone system has been set up in the Region to keep paddlers informed about all the local events:

0423 711531

Any club who would like to have information put on the line should get in touch with Marianne Spender on 0422 882908.

Canoe Clubs in the Yorkshire and Humberside Region

The following is a list of BCU Affiliated Clubs in the Region. Each club is coded (see following page) to indicate its main activities:

Acomb Christian Fellow	H N
Bradford and Bingley C.C.	B E F H N S T V X
Calderdale Youth C.C.	B F H J K M N S T V W X
Dales C.C.	B F H J N S V X
Dewsbury Adventure Club	A B E H J M N S T V X
Giggleswick C.C.	B H J I N S T
Glanford and Scunthorpe C.C.	A B C F H N S T V W X
Grimsby Cleethorpes C.C.	A B C F H K M N S T V W X
Halifax C.C.	B F H J N S T V X
Hollowford Centre	H J N X
Hull and District C.C.	A B C F H J K N S T V W X
Humbersiders	F S
Humberside Ladies Canoe Polo Club	F
Keighley (Fell Lane) Scout Group	N V
Kingston Kayak Club	A B C E F H J K M N S T V W X
Leeds C.C.	A B E F H J K L M N S T V X
Pennine C.C.	A B E F H J K M S X
Sheffield C.C.	A B C E F H J K L M N S T V W X

Sheffield University C.C.	A B D E J M N P T X
South Shore Paddlers	A B F J K N S V X
Swaledale Outdoor Club.	B G H J K L M N S T V W X
Trent Valley C.C.	B D F M N S T V W X
West Yorkshire C.C.	A B C E F H J K L M N S T V X
White Rose C.C. (Leeds)	B E F H J K L M N S T V W X
York C.C.	B E H J L N X

Due to frequent changes of club secretaries, these have not been included. You are advised to contact the BCU for up-to-date information.

Details of the BCU codes used are as follows:

A MARATHON
B SLALOM
C RACING
D SURF EVENTS
E WILD WATER RACES
F CANOE POLO
G CANOE SAILING
H TOURING INLAND (PLACID)
J TOURING INLAND (WHITE WATER)
K TOURING SEA
L FOREIGN TOURING
M SURFING
N GENERAL RECREATION
P MAJOR EXPEDITIONS
R CANOE LIFEGUARD CORPS
S INTRODUCTORY COURSES (INDOOR)
T ROLLING COURSE (INDOOR)
V INTRODUCTORY COURSES (OUTDOOR)
W ROLLING COURSES (OUTDOOR)
X ENCOURAGES PARTICIPATION OF DISABLED PERSONS

Canoeing Equipment from Wild Water

Over the years a great deal of support has been given to the Yorkshire and Humberside Region by Chris Hawkesworth of Wild Water.

Wild Water manufacture and retail a complete range of quality canoeing equipment at competitive prices. Their own retail outlet at Pateley Bridge near Harrogate is open 9:00am to 5:00pm, Mondays to Fridays and Saturdays by appointment.

For further details of current products and prices contact:

Wild Water (Montbell U.K.)
The Mill
Glasshouses
Pateley Bridge
HARROGATE HG3 5QH
(Tel 0423 711624)

Canoeing at Sleningford Watermill

Sleningford Watermill is home to a well established caravan and camping park within a beautiful riverside area and described by the Yorkshire Tourist Authority as making the most of the natural environment. The park is open for camping from April to October, but in its unique position it is able to offer year round facilities for canoeing on a daily basis.

An ideal white water stretch presents a challenge to all levels of competence depending on the state of the river at the time. For some years the site has hosted a very successful National Division 4/5 Slalom Competition in the month of September.

Situated alongside the river, just off the A6108, 5 miles north of Ripon, the site has parking facilities, for which a fee is charged, changing facilities and toilets and a variety of access points to the river. The campsite shop sells a limited range of canoeing equipment and hot and cold refreshments are also available.

For further information contact:

Mrs Francis Petchey
Sleningford Watermill
North Stainley
RIPON HG4 3HQ
(Tel 0765 635201)

Weil's Disease

WHAT IS IT?
Weil's disease is a bacterial infection carried in rats urine which contaminates water and wet river banks. The bacteria do not survive for long in dry conditions. The risk of infection is greater where stagnant or slow moving water is involved, but cases have occurred on swift moving streams as well as lowland rivers. There is an enhanced risk following a flash flood where rats' runs are washed out.

HOW SERIOUS IS IT?
It can be a serious illness requiring hospital treatment and can lead to kidney or liver failure. One patient in 19 dies with it. Weil's Disease is a notifiable illness.

HOW DO I CATCH IT?
The bacteria are absorbed through the skin and mucous membranes of the mouth and eyes. It gets into the blood stream more easily if you have a minor cut on your skin or feet or if you do capsize drill or rolling.

WHAT SHOULD I DO ABOUT IT?
If you feel ill after canoeing, particularly from 3 to 19 days following, and have any of the features described in the case history CALL YOUR DOCTOR EARLY. The most common early symptoms are: temperature, an influenza-like illness and joint and muscle pains (pains in the calf muscles are often particularly noticeable). Jaundice and/or conjunctivitis may be present, or develop, although the absence of any of these symptoms does not mean that the illness is not Weil's Disease- nor does a symptom in isolation necessarily indicate that Weil's Disease is present.

TELL YOUR DOCTOR YOU HAVE BEEN CANOEING AND WHERE. IF WEIL'S DISEASE IS SUSPECTED, ANTIBIOTICS MUST BE ADMINISTERED IMMEDIATELY- WITHIN 24-48 HOURS OF ONSET. A BLOOD TEST SHOULD BE UNDERTAKEN TO CONFIRM THIS NOTIFIABLE ILLNESS. IF THE LOCAL PUBLIC HEALTH LABORATORY IS NOT EQUIPPED TO UNDER-TAKE AN ELISA TEST THE SAMPLE SHOULD BE SENT DIRECT TO THE LEPTOSPIROSIS REFERENCE UNIT AT HEREFORD.

IN SUMMARY
* Avoid capsize drill/rolling in stagnant or slow moving water.
* Wash or shower after canoeing.
* Cover minor scratches on exposed parts of the body with water-proof plaster.
* Use foot-wear to avoid cutting feet.
* If you have flu-like illness after canoeing go to your GP early – tell him you are a canoeist.

EARLY IDENTIFICATION OF THE ILLNESS IS VITAL.

YOUR DOCTOR IS REMINDED OF THE EXISTENCE OF:

The Leptospirosis Reference Unit
Public Health Laboratory
County Hospital
HEREFORD HR1 2ER

RESULTS OF BLOOD TESTS HAVE BEEN KNOWN TO TAKE 2-3 WEEKS THROUGH THE NORMAL LABORATORY SYSTEM. WATER SPORTS PERSONS HAVE BEEN BECOME SERIOUSLY ILL, AND SOME HAVE EVEN DIED, THROUGH SLOW DIAGNOSIS AND TREATMENT SINCE 1987. THE LOCAL PUBLIC HEALTH LABORATORY SHOULD BE EQUIPPED TO UNDERTAKE AN ELISA TEST, FROM WHICH A RESULT CAN BE OBTAINED WITHIN 3 HOURS OF COMMENCEMENT. OTHERWISE THE SAMPLE SHOULD BE SENT TO THE LEPTOSPIROSIS REFERENCE UNIT AT HEREFORD.

Disclaimer

Information contained in this guide does not imply a legal right to canoe any of the rivers described or a right of access to these rivers.

Canoeing is an inherently dangerous sport and any person, especially if inexperienced, should approach it with caution and under appropriate supervision.

The information given in this publication is intended as a general guide under favourable river conditions and should not be considered as a guarantee of safe passage. It is the sole responsibility of the individual to decide whether a descent is within their capability. Weirs can present grave hazards to canoeists and should be inspected and only be descended under safe conditions.

The authors and publisher of this guide cannot accept responsibility for any accidents, injury, or loss suffered by any reader of this book however these may be caused.

Use of the guide

Both the maps and the commentary start at the highest point in a river where canoeing is normally possible and describe the major features of the river. However, where features occur close together, some have been omitted.

All maps noted in the commentaries refer to the ORDNANCE SURVEY 1:50 000 LANDRANGER SERIES.

For all appropriate points where there are features of interest to the canoeist, Ordnance Survey grid references have been given. These consist of three sections: the 100 000 metre grid square, the EASTINGS and the NORTHINGS.

The 100 000 metre grid square is quoted first and shows the area in which the point lies, for example 'SE' or 'NY'.

The eastings are then quoted; these are given for vertical lines running south-north and consist of a three digit number of which the first two digits show the western border of the 1000 metre square; the third digit is an estimate, in 100 metre units from the west side of the square.

The northings are quoted last; these are given for horizontal lines running west-east and consist of a three digit number of which the first two digits show the southern border of the 1000 metre square; the third digit is an estimate, in 100 metre units from the south side of the square.

For example, the bridge at Burnsall has the grid reference [SE 033612].

Use of the guide

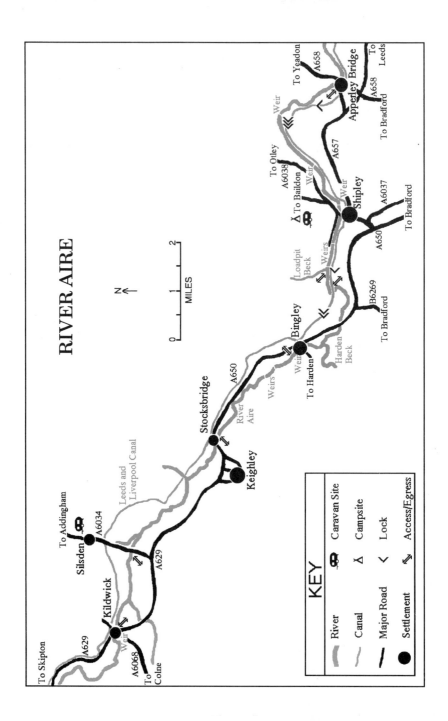

RIVER AIRE

GENERAL DESCRIPTION

The River Aire is reputedly canoeable from its source to the sea, but this is only possible as a stunt when in high spate. It is normally canoeable from the junction with Earby Beck. The lower parts of the river are now subject to much less industrial pollution than in previous years and in passing through Keighley, Bingley, Shipley and Leeds provide an interesting insight into Yorkshire's industrial heritage.

Upper Aire

GRADE: 0 - I plus weirs.

REMARKS: The river is canoed regularly.

MAPS REQUIRED: LANDRANGER 103 and 104.

ACCESS INFORMATION: There are no access agreements.

LOCAL ACCESS OFFICER: John Ackroyd
Edge Bottom
Denholme
BRADFORD BD13 4JW
(Tel 0274 832850)

ITINERARY:

Miles

0   Junction with Earby Beck [SD 962515]. The road to Carleton from the A59 Skipton–Gisburn road initially passes close to the river and provides possible access points.

1½   Carleton Bridge [SD 984501]. Access is possible here.

2¼   Railway bridge.

4¼   Cononley Bridge.

6¼   Kildwick Bridge and Weir (shallow). Access is by way of the gate on the Kildwick side of the river [SE 012457].

8   Silsden Bridge [SE 039451]. Access is by way of the stile on the right hand side of the bridge.

10½   Holden Park Bridge.

12¼   Stock Bridge [SE 075423]. Access is from the A650: opposite the Bridge Hotel on the north side of the bridge turn into Cornwall Road, then turn left into Florist Street and continue to the end. Unload canoes and carry them over the rough ground veering left down to the river. This is the usual starting point for day trips down the river. Please do not obstruct local residents parking.

14½   Marley railway bridge.

15   Marley Weir. This should be inspected and portaged on the left bank if necessary.

15¼ Castlefields Weir. This is normally shot towards the left, avoiding the large rock close to the wall on the left immediately after the weir.

16 Bingley Weir [SE 105394]. There is not usually enough water to shoot this, but shoot at the centre when possible. You can easily carry your canoe over the weir or land on the right bank. Access is from the A650: take the B6429 Harden road by the Parish Church, cross the river, turn right and then right again behind the houses back to the river. It is possible to park on the left but do not block the track as it is well used. Avoid the gate on the extreme left hand side as this is often blocked.

16 Bingley Bridge.

16½ Myrtle Park and Harden Beck. Pass to the right of the island. There is an obstruction in the bed of the river which can be awkward in low water. A footbridge is to be found at the end of the island.

17¼ Cottingley Bridge. About 500 yards below this bridge there is a shingle bank which sets the current sharply into the left bank, where trees over-hang. Take care with any beginners.

18¼ Hirstwood Railway Bridge. Below the bridge there is a left hand bend followed by a broken weir and stepping stones.

18½ Seven Arches Canal Aqueduct [SE 123383]. This carries the canal over the river. You can return to Bingley by the canal, landing just below the bridge on the right bank.

19½ Hirst Mill Weir [SE 130384]. Bradford Rowing Club use this section of the river and the landing stage is their property. This is the usual place to leave the river since it becomes badly polluted below Shipley. Hirst Weir can be shot but should be inspected. In low water, shoot it slowly on the left. In medium and high water a stopper forms.

20 Roberts Park. Saltaire. This is a public boating section, so beware of mugs in boats. Salts Mill Weir can be shot on the right down the concrete chute, or in the centre in low water.

20½ Baildon Bridge and Weir. This is usually shot on the right but should be inspected.

21¼ Railway Bridge.

22¼ Buck Mill Bridge and Weir. This can be shot in the centre in low water or on the extreme right in high water.

23 Esholt Sewage Works. A weir follows the bridge and should be inspected.

24½ Footbridge.

24¾ Rail Bridge [SE 191386].

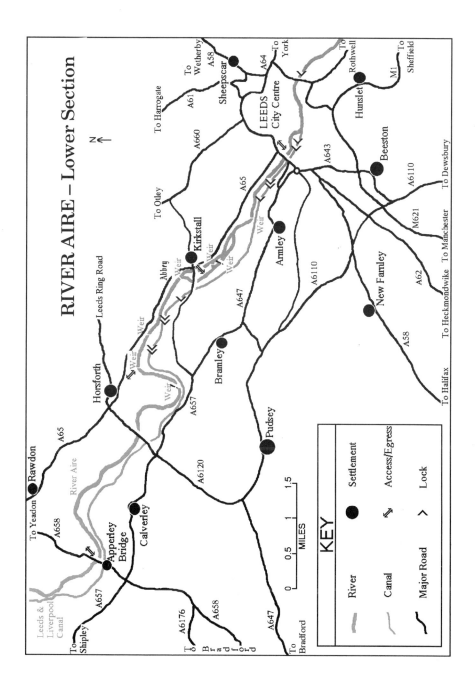

RIVER AIRE – Lower Section

N

KEY

River

Canal

Major Road

Settlement

Access/Egress

Lock

MILES

0   0,5   1   1,5

3

Lower Aire

GRADE:	0 - I plus weirs.
REMARKS:	The river is canoed regularly.
MAP REQUIRED:	LANDRANGER 104.
ACCESS INFORMATION:	There are no access agreements.
LOCAL ACCESS OFFICER:	Norman Taylor 73 Gateland Lane Shadwell LEEDS LS17 8LN (Tel 0532 737393)

ITINERARY

Miles

25   Apperley Bridge [SE 195380]. There are two bridges here, about 50 yards apart. Leave the river by either bank before the first bridge since the second bridge is often badly obstructed by debris.

26   Rail Bridge.

27   Rail Viaduct.

31½   Horsforth Road Bridge. Leeds ring-road.

32½   Large weir. This is only shootable in low water and is very dangerous when the river is up. Portage is possible on the left bank, but difficult.

33   Newlay bridge and railway bridge [SE 239369]. These are followed immediately by Newlay Weir. The weir can be shot either in the centre or towards the right hand side depending on the river level. Portage on the right bank; egress on the left hand side.

33½   Kirkstall Forge Weir. This broken weir is best taken on the extreme right although the centre is possible with a wiggle!

34¼   Kirkstall Abbey and Weir. Shoot anywhere right of centre, avoiding the bushes and brambles on the bank.

35   Headingley Rugby Club- Leeds Canoe Club site [SE 262353]. Egress is possible on the left hand side.

35¼   Ford. This can be shot either in the centre or towards the right hand side. Care should be taken to avoid the stakes.

35½   Boomer Weir. This is the big one: a horse shoe weir with side walls. Inspection is vital since it may be shot at low water only and is very dangerous even if the river is only running modestly! Shoot on the left about 12 - 15 ft out from the bank.

36½   Museum Weir. This may be shot on the extreme left.

37   Road and rail bridges.

37½   Leeds City Centre [SE 297333]. Dark Arches: 'The Black Hole' is not for the faint-hearted. You must take either the third or fourth arch from the right, the others are blind. It is dark and noisy but reasonable at low water. Egress is possible on the right hand side.

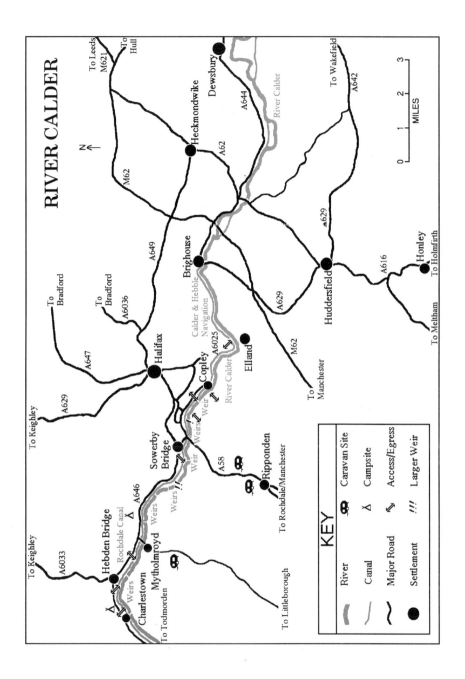

RIVER CALDER

KEY

River		Caravan Site
Canal	Λ	Campsite
Major Road		Access/Egress
Settlement	///	Larger Weir

RIVER CALDER

GRADE:	I - II plus weirs. The river is best in moderate to high water.
REMARKS:	The river is canoed regularly and is a navigation below Sowerby Bridge.
MAPS REQUIRED:	LANDRANGER 103 and 104.
ACCESS INFORMATION:	There are no access agreements.
LOCAL ACCESS OFFICER:	David Gent Flat 68, Smeaton Gardens 18 Milford Street HUDDERSFIELD HD1 3DY (Tel 0484 518913)

GENERAL DESCRIPTION

The River Calder flows through a picturesque valley with a multitude of interesting natural and man-made features. Particularly notable for its industrial heritage with the different stages of development being particularly noticeable from the river. For many years the river has suffered from industrial pollution but improved awareness and the drastic reduction of local industry have benefited the river to the extent that trout and other fish have reappeared over the last few years. Whilst still not the crystal clear water of the Dales rivers, the pollution is at a level acceptable to most canoeists. There are numerous access points throughout its length and the adjacent canals allow for some interesting two-way trips. Down stream of Elland the river is less interesting and more polluted. Much of its route is canalised except where the fairly frequent weirs force the canal through locks.

ITINERARY

Miles

0   Charlestown [SD 972264]. Access is possible over a bridge just below a vertical weir. Canoeing upstream of here is considered impractical.

½   300 yard long tunnel. There is an interesting rock garden in the middle.

1   Hebden Bridge [SD 991271]. The River Hebden enters on the left. There is good access from the car park in the middle of Hebden Bridge onto the river. The low bridge is normally best taken through the left hand archway.

1½   Hebden Bridge Weir. The weir can be shot by sliding down the abutments but this would be hard on your boat.

2   Scott's Garage [SE 004265]. This is the most often used starting point for trips on the Calder. Access is over a low wall. There are small stoppers, offering surprises to novices, but these are quickly washed out in high water.

2¼   Mytholmroyd. The River Elphin enters on the right. There are two bridges here.

3¼   Brearley Weir. This should be shot in the centre. The water below the weir is canoeable in most conditions but forms very large standing waves in flood.

4¼   Luddenden Foot. Boy Bridge and Boy Bridge Weir. This is a collapsed weir, providing a potentially interesting rapid. There is an obvious route down the left hand side, avoiding the retaining wall. The weir can be portaged on the right.

4¾   Weir. This was originally V-shaped but has collapsed on the right. It should be shot in the centre.

5   Double weir. This consists of a large weir followed almost immediately by a smaller weir. The first is best taken on the right and the second one either through the slot in the centre or on the left hand side. In flood conditions, horrendous stoppers form below these weirs. They can be portaged on the left bank, around the far side of the mill.

5¾   Holling Mill Weir [SE 053240]. Access/egress is on the left hand side. The weir can be shot close to either bank although the left hand side is best.

6¼   Puzzle Hall Inn [SE 057237]. The ladder on the left bank allows egress for refreshments.

6¾   Sowerby Bridge [SE 060235]. The weir presents no problems. The River Ryburn enters on the right. Halifax Canoe Club, with its artificial slalom course and club house, is situated here.

7   Cast Iron Bridge [SE 067237]. This is thought to be the second oldest bridge of its kind in the world after Iron Bridge. Just prior to the bridge, access can be easily gained to the Calder and Hebble Navigation Canal.

7¼   Mearclough Weir. This should be shot on the left in low water and on the right in high water. It builds a large wall to wall canoe gobbler. Portage is difficult but it is possible to use the canal, regaining the river over the next bridge.

7¼   Mearclough Bridge [SE 070237]. Access is on the right.

7¾   Stern Mill Bridge and Weir (Standard Wire Works). Access is through the mill yard. The weir is arrow shaped and can be shot on the right, with a steep or vertical drop into deep water, or in the centre, which is less exciting but harder on your boat.

8¼   Railway viaducts. There are two of these.

8½   Copley rapids [SE 084225]. Access is possible at several points. This is the site of the Copley Village slalom competition.

10¼   Elland Bridge and Elland rapids [SE 108215]. Egress is on the left hand side.

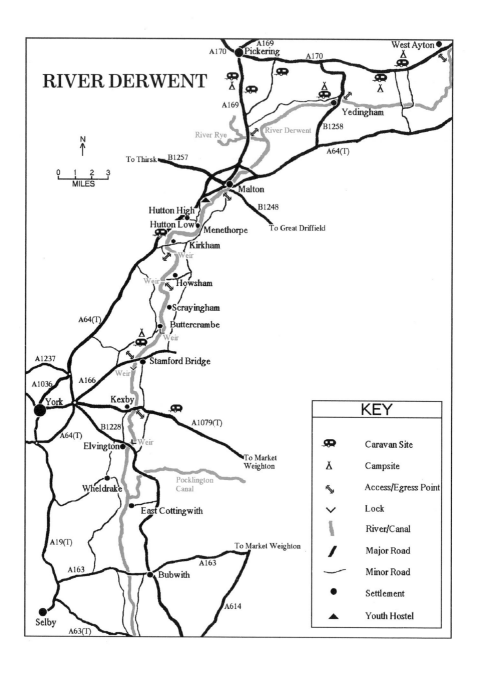

RIVER DERWENT

N

0 1 2 3
MILES

KEY

🚐	Caravan Site
Ⴟ	Campsite
↕	Access/Egress Point
∨	Lock
	River/Canal
/	Major Road
—	Minor Road
●	Settlement
▲	Youth Hostel

West Ayton

A169
Pickering
A170
A170

A169

Yedingham
B1258

River Rye   River Derwent

A64(T)

To Thirsk B1257

Malton

B1248

Hutton High

Hutton Low Menethorpe   To Great Driffield

Kirkham
Weir

Weir Howsham

Scrayingham

A64(T)

Buttercrambe
Weir

Stamford Bridge

A1237

A166

Weir

A1036

York   Kexby

A1079(T)

A64(T)   B1228

Elvington Weir

To Market
Weighton

Pocklington
Canal

Wheldrake

East Cottingwith

A19(T)

To Market Weighton

A163

A163
Bubwith

A614

Selby

A63(T)

RIVER DERWENT

GRADE:	I.
REMARKS:	The river is tidal from Elvington.
MAPS REQUIRED:	LANDRANGER 100, 101 and 105.
ACCESS INFORMATION:	There are no access agreements but the river is canoed regularly.
LOCAL ACCESS OFFICER:	Neil Sanderson 8 Dean Road Norton MALTON YO17 9BX

GENERAL DESCRIPTION

The Derwent rises on Fylingdale Moor and flows south-east through Hackness and the Forge valley to within 4 miles of the sea at Scarborough. Then the river turns inland and follows the Vale of Pickering westwards to join the Rye. The Derwent turns south and flows through Malton and Stamford Bridge to join the Ouse at Barmby-on-the-Marsh. Tidal from Elvington, the river is described from where it emerges from the Forge Valley at West Ayton.

ITINERARY
Miles

0	West Ayton [SE 988848]. The river follows a winding channel for the next 6 miles.
6	Ganton [SE 978790]. The course of the river has been straightened for the next 5 miles.
7	Bridge.
7½	Bridge.
11	Foulbridge. There is no public access.
13	Yedingham Bridge [SE 893796]. This is a good starting place.
18	Marishes Railway Bridge.
20	Confluence with the River Rye [SE 825757]. Howe Bridge, 1 mile upstream on the River Rye, is a good starting point.
23	Old Malton.
24	Malton [SE 786715]. If starting or finishing here, you should access/egress by the last bridge. Parking is possible in the station yard.
25	Derwent Bank Youth Hostel.
27	Cherry Islands.
30	Castle Howard School.
31	Kirkham Abbey [SE 735657]. There is a bridge and weir, and an access/egress point.
34	Howsham Weir and Bridge [SE 730629]. There is an access/egress point.
37	Buttercrambe. Here there is a disused lock, weir and bridge.
40	Stamford Bridge [SE 712556]. The site includes a weir, lock, access/egress point and campsite.
43½	Kexby Bridge on the A1079 [SE 705512]. Access/egress is possible here.
46	Elvington Bridge. The lock and weir can be portaged on the right bank.

50	East Cottingwith. Pocklington Canal joins the river here. The river is now tidal.
55	Bubwith Bridge.
60	Loftsome Bridge.
62	Confluence with the River Ouse [SE 678288].

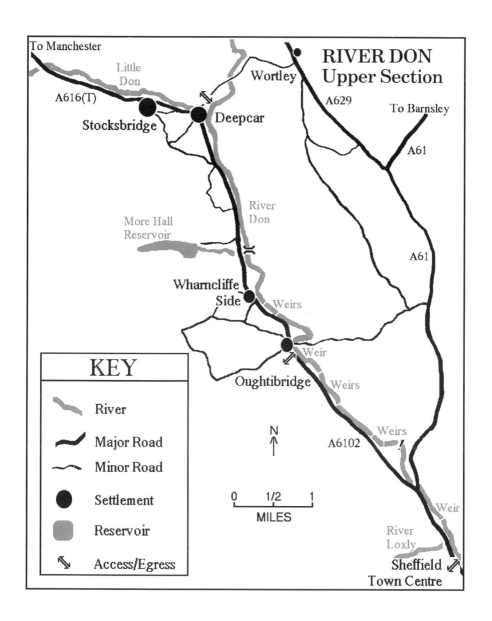

RIVER DON
Upper Section

To Manchester

Little Don

Wortley

A616(T)

A629

To Barnsley

Stocksbridge

Deepcar

A61

River Don

More Hall Reservoir

A61

Wharncliffe Side

Weirs

Weir

Oughtibridge

Weirs

KEY

~~~ River

~~~ Major Road

~~~ Minor Road

● Settlement

▮ Reservoir

↗ Access/Egress

N
↑

Weirs

A6102

0   1/2   1
MILES

Weir

River Loxly

Sheffield ↗
Town Centre

11

RIVER DON

GRADE:	II - III plus weirs.
REMARKS:	The river is canoed regularly and is best in moderate to high water.
MAP REQUIRED:	LANDRANGER 110.
ACCESS INFORMATION:	Access agreements are currently under negotiation.
LOCAL ACCESS OFFICER:	Mark Steel 11 Watkinson Gardens SHEFFIELD S19 6LU (Tel 0742 474696)

GENERAL DESCRIPTION

The River Don rises on Thurlstone Moor and flows through Wharncliffe Crags towards Sheffield. The upper stretch of the river is only canoeable in high water, being narrow and fast flowing; it is also relatively clean. The Lower Don has many tributaries, which ensure a year round supply of canoeable water. Levels of pollution have fallen dramatically in recent years, resulting in the return of fish and wildlife to this urban river. For much of its course the river flows through woodland and, as a result, trees are swept into the river. FALLEN TREES ARE A POTENTIAL HAZARD AND CARE SHOULD BE TAKEN.

The middle section can be paddled at high to moderate levels and is suitable for proficiency level paddlers led by a more experienced paddler.

The lower Don is only suitable in moderate to low water, as most of the weirs are large and dangerous and bordered by long high walls which completely prevent portage or egress.

ITINERARY
UPPER DON

Miles
0	Deepcar, Station Road Bridge [SK 292981]. Access is by the public footpath running on the right bank, upstream of the bridge. 200 yards below this point the Little Don enters on the right.
1	Start of the gorge section in which there are many submerged rocks.
1¼	The small pipe outlet on the left marks the start of the double 'Rockgarden'. Inspect this from the A616 via the grass verge on the near side of the road. In moderate water both sections require accurate paddling in between the rocks. In high water the first section of rocks is washed out, but the second section forms a V-shaped stopper with a submerged boulder at the end of the 'V'!
1¾	Private bridge and confluence of More Hall Reservoir outlet.
2	Large island midstream which should be passed on the left hand side.
2½	Broken weir. This weir should be inspected and can be easily portaged on the left bank or shot near the centre.

2¾   Large weir. Inspect this weir, which can be portaged on the left bank. There is a large stopper in high water.

3½   Tissue works. Pass smartly through, but beware of low branches. The somewhat colourful pollution is harmless and biodegradable.

4   Oughtibridge Bridge and Weir [SK 308935]. Inspect the weir and shoot via the centre section if desired. Note that egress can be made to the footpath on the left bank. Beware of the trees on the right hand side.

MIDDLE SECTION

4¼   Access can be made from the footpath on the left bank after the weir [SK 308935].

4½   Weir. Shoot this in the centre since there is a large stopper on the right hand side. 100 yards further on there are some rapids with submerged boulders. These can be portaged on the left bank.

5   Weir. After the house on the right bank the river swings left around a stone barrage and then takes a sharp right turn over a small vertical weir, which should be inspected. Beware of overhanging trees and wooden stakes on the right before the weir. This can be portaged on the left bank.

5½   Small weir.

5¾   Weir. This can be shot in the centre or portaged on either bank.

6   Large Tower Block on the right hand side [SK 329915]. The river then sweeps round a right hand bend before an IMPOSSIBLE AND VERY DANGEROUS 15 ft VERTICAL WEIR. Portage can be made on the right bank.

6¾   Leppings Lane Bridge.

7   Penistone Lane Bridge.

7½   Clubmill Lane Bridge. There is a small broken weir.

7¾   Large weir. Shoot this in the centre, or portage on the left bank.

8   Confluence with the River Loxley, which enters from the right.

8¼   Clubmill Road [SK 343893]. Access/egress is possible here. 100 yards downstream, there is a weir which should be shot in the centre.

LOWER DON

INSPECT ALL WEIRS

8½   Neepend Lane Bridge [SK 343889].

8¾   Weir. Shoot this on the left, but beware of overhanging trees, debris, submerged millstones and metal pillars.

9   Rutland Road Bridge.

9¼   Bridge and weir. The weir should be shot on the left, via the left hand archway of the bridge, and you should keep to the left hand channel.

9½   Corporation Street Bridge.

9¾   Weir and bridge. This weir should be shot about 1/3 of the way out from the left hand side. Following this, there are some steel pillars on the right and then a stone bridge.

10   Large viaduct.

10¼   Weir. This weir can be very dangerous in flood. In lower water conditions, shoot on the left hand side and then take the left channel.

10½   Weir. This can be shot in the centre, taking the left channel although attention should be paid to the steel plates on the wall after the weir.

11   Attercliffe Road Bridge.

11¼   Bridge. 100 yards below this bridge, there is a weir which should be shot on the right, taking the right channel.

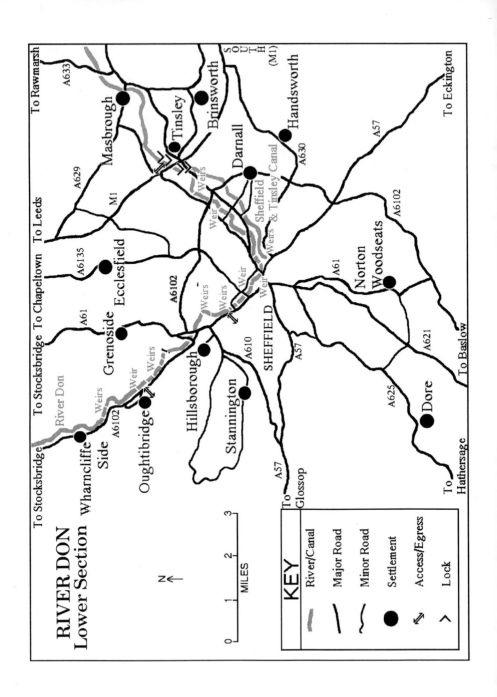

RIVER DON
Lower Section

N

KEY

| River/Canal |
| Major Road |
| Minor Road |
| Settlement |
| Access/Egress |
| Lock |

MILES
0 1 2 3

11½ Stevenson Road Bridge.
11¾ Newhall Street Bridge.
12¼ Hawke Street Bridge.
12½ Weir. This weir is large and steep but can be shot in the centre, noting the metal stakes on the left hand side.
12¾ Weedan Street Bridge.
13½ Weir. Shoot this weir in the centre.

There are several new bridges to the new shopping centre on the right. Follow the river to the M1 viaduct and egress on the right hand side just past the motorway. There are some concrete steps up to the navigation tow-path [SK 398911].

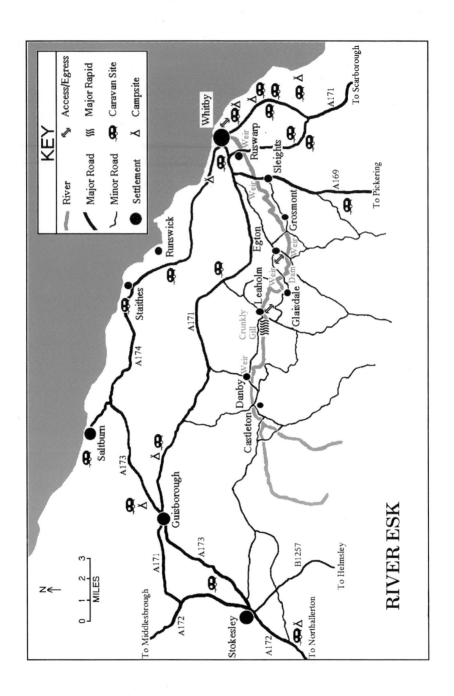

RIVER ESK

RIVER ESK

GRADE:　　　　　　　　　　III - IV in high water.

REMARKS:　　　　　　　　The river is seldom canoed and is best in high water. The Esk is very overgrown above Lealholm and is tidal below Ruswarp Weir. Near Grosmont there is a good deal of fishing activity.

MAP REQUIRED:　　　　　LANDRANGER 94.

ACCESS INFORMATION:　There are no access agreements.

LOCAL ACCESS OFFICER:　Don Raspin
28 Cotswold Drive
Skelton
CLEVELAND TS12 2JN
(Tel 0287 650668)

GENERAL DESCRIPTION

This little river, which empties into the sea at Whitby, has been canoed from as high up as Castleton in high water. One stretch, Crunkly Gill, has been described as grade IV in high water conditions. The stretch between Glaisdale and Egton Bridge also provides good water after heavy rain. Below Sleights the river becomes a navigation. Beware of fallen trees above Egton Bridge.

ITINERARY

Miles

0　　　Castleton [NZ 685085]. Access is possible here.
1　　　Road bridge.
2　　　Danby Mill Weir. The weir can be shot or portaged on the right bank. The river then passes under a road bridge.
2½　　Railway bridge.
3　　　Danby Lodge and Footbridge.
3¾　　Railway bridge followed by a road bridge.
4½　　Little Fryup Beck enters on the right. Following this, there is a bridge.
4¾　　Road bridge.
5　　　Footbridge.
5¾　　Great Fryup Beck enters on the right.
7　　　Crunkly Gill [NZ 754071]. This wooded gorge is grade IV in spate with huge boulders and rapidly falling water. A route has to be forged rather than found.
8¼　　Lealholm Bridge [NZ 763076]. Access/egress can be made here.
10　　　Rake Farm. Railway and road bridge.
11　　　Glaisdale Weir. Shoot the weir in the centre.
11½　　Dam. Portage must be made on the left for 50 yards. There now follows a 1 mile long grade III section strewn with boulders.
13½　　Egton Bridge Weir [NZ 802053]. Shoot this weir but beware of spikes, or portage on the left bank. Access/egress is possible here.
15¾　　Grosmont. In the next section there are 7 railway bridges.

20½ Sleights Weir. It is normal to portage this on the right bank, but experts can shoot the weir on the overflow when it is clear of driftwood.

22   Ruswarp Weir. Shoot the weir or portage on the left bank.

23   Glen Esk Campsite is on the right bank [NZ 894096].

24½ Whitby Harbour.

24¾ Bridge and outer harbour [NZ 900110]. There is a small beach on the right hand side and a slipway and car park can be found on the right, above the bridge.

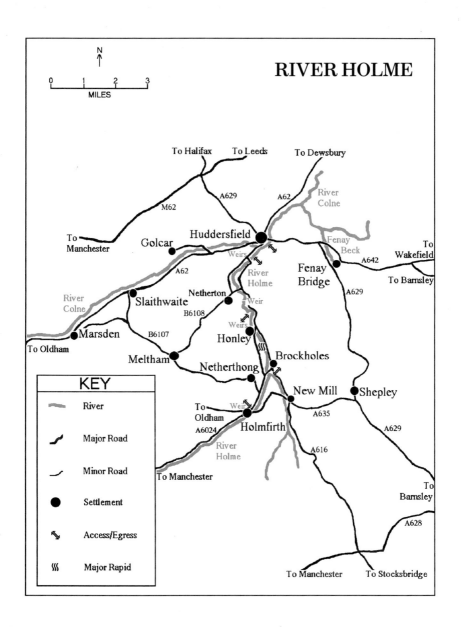

RIVER HOLME

GRADE:	I - III plus weirs.
REMARKS:	The river is canoed regularly.
MAP REQUIRED:	LANDRANGER 110.
ACCESS INFORMATION:	There are no access agreements.
LOCAL ACCESS OFFICER:	Barry Gray 17 Benomley Road Almondbury HUDDERSFIELD HD5 8LR (Tel 0484 544196)

GENERAL DESCRIPTION

The River Holme starts life on the moors above the 'Last of the Summer Wine' Village of Holmfirth and winds its way north down the Holme Valley until it reaches its confluence with the River Colne in Huddersfield and ultimately the River Calder. The best section is between Brockholes and Honley with grades from I to III depending on water level. Although not technically difficult the River must be taken seriously, the dangers being blind, narrow bends and the ever present risk of fallen trees. This river has its share of weirs, some presenting a great risk to life and limb. These are noted in more detail in the following itinerary. Some have not been mentioned at all to maintain interest but all should be inspected. Because of the above mentioned dangers this river is not for the inexperienced.

As the river quality has been improved over the past few years, so the anglers have started to appear in small numbers. Although no problems have been experienced, please treat them with our usual courtesy.

The River Holme, like most Pennine rivers, rises and falls very quickly and at low water is not worth attempting if you respect the bottom of your canoe. The river is best shot at above low to medium water.

ITINERARY:

Miles

0   Access is made behind Holmfirth Swimming Pool (next to the Police Station) on the A6024 [SE 147092]. Start your trip above or below a small Horse Shoe Weir (but see below).

¾   Brockholes [SE 151109]. Access/egress can be made here, if the water is suspected to be low this is the best place to start. To find the access point, go through Brockholes on the A616 and head towards New Mill for ½ mile, then turn right and go to the bottom of the hill (100 yards). Access is made above the footbridge on the right.

1¾   Bungalow Section. This is probably the best section of the river, with an interesting stopper at the bottom that can be dangerous in high water. Note that there may be barbed wire across the river just past this stopper. This section can be grade III in the right conditions.

2¼   Honley. After the road bridge at Honley, there is a large Horse Shoe Weir which should be shot tight left. DO NOT shoot this weir in the centre since here a large concrete block awaits the unwary. A second weir lies 100 yards below which can also be difficult. Again shoot this on the left hand side. A whirlpool can usually be found on the right which gets bigger and stronger the higher the water. A short section of grade II follows and a small river enters from the left.

2¾   Access/egress can be made under a small road bridge, ending the Brockholes to Honley section [SE 141128].

3¼   The next weir comes on a right hand bend, usually portaged on the right bank [SE 138128]. DO NOT SHOOT THIS WEIR, A CONCRETE BASE guarantees A FEET IN THE HEAD TRANSPLANT.

6   Access/egress can be made under a road bridge [SE 142157]. 100 yards downstream, there is a double weir which can be a real nasty in medium to high water. The sides of the river bank are high and a retreat could be difficult. Rescues would be interesting if not impossible. CHECK THE WATER LEVEL BEFORE REACHING THIS POINT. If pushed to it, a very narrow 'V' can be found in the centre in medium plus water but at high water, forget it.

6¼   Confluence with the River Colne [SE 143159]. Egress can be made on the right, at about 500 yards past the road bridge.

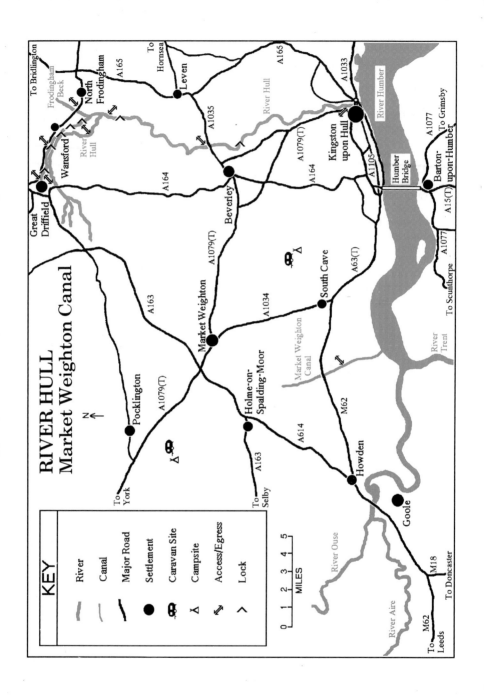

RIVER HULL
Market Weighton Canal

KEY

River	
Canal	
Major Road	
Settlement	●
Caravan Site	
Campsite	
Access/Egress	
Lock	

MILES

0 1 2 3 4 5

N

To Bridlington

To Hornsea

Frodingham Beck

North Frodingham

A165

Leven

A165

A1033

River Humber

River Hull

Wansford

River Hull

A1035

A1079(T)

Kingston upon Hull

A1077

To Grimsby

Great Driffield

A164

Beverley

A164

A1105

Humber Bridge

Barton-upon-Humber

A15(T)

A1079(T)

Market Weighton

A1034

South Cave

A63(T)

A1077

To Scunthorpe

A163

A1079(T)

Pocklington

Holme-on-Spalding-Moor

Market Weighton Canal

River Trent

M62

A614

Howden

Goole

River Ouse

M18

To Doncaster

River Aire

To Leeds

M62

To York

A163

To Selby

RIVER HULL

GRADE:	0 - I
REMARKS:	The river is canoed regularly although the upper section of the river should be avoided due to trout fishing.
MAP REQUIRED:	LANDRANGER 107.
ACCESS INFORMATION:	There are no access agreements.
LOCAL ACCESS OFFICER:	Ted Smith 4 Wilton Terrace HORNSEA HU18 1PX (Tel 0964 534393)

GENERAL DESCRIPTION

In general canoeists should avoid the upper section of the River Hull. The upper part near Wansford is a stretch used for trout fishing for which licences are bought and canoeists would not be welcome. Best points of access are at Brigham (very limited parking), the east bank (not easy), Frodingham landing (good access point), near Hull Bridge and the Hull and District landing. On no account should the pub car park be used here. Make sure to keep to the public footpath on the east side near the bridge. The Beverley Beck situation is still under negotiation. There is no easy egress from the river at present.

ITINERARY

Miles

0   Canal Head [TA 028573]. Access and parking are available at the Canal Head Wharf.

½   Town Lock [TA 031569]. The lock provides an alternative starting point. Portage past the lock on the west bank through a section of fence which unbolts, then across the lawn of the bungalow and alongside the bank. This is a public right of way. All other lock portages are on the east bank.

1½   Whin Hill Lock [TA 051568]. The access point is on the east bank.

2½   Wansford Lock and Bridge. This is best portaged as one bridge is very low and becomes impassable in high water.

3   Snakeholme Lock and Bridge.

4   Brigham Bridge [TA 077537]. The access point is on the east bank.

5   Junction with Frodingham Beck. Frodingham Bridge is 1 mile upstream from here [TA 083527]. Public access is available at the wharf (part of the Driffield canal) on the left bank just south of the bridge. Upstream of the bridge the water is in private hands.

5½   Junction with River Hull. The Hull can be navigated 2 miles upstream as far as Corpse Landing, where there is a nature reserve. We are asked not to land or launch from here.

6   Bethels Bridge [TA 079510]. Access is from the east bank above and west bank below the bridge.

7   Struncheon Hill Lock. Portage on the west bank. Below these locks the river becomes tidal.

9   Baswick Landing. This is to be found on the east side.

10   Wilfholme Landing. This lies on the west side.

11   Aike Beck.

11½   Leven Canal. The entrance to this canal is blocked.

12   Arram.

14½   Tickton by-pass bridge (A1035) and Hull Bridge [TA 055417]. Access is possible here.

16   Grovehill Bridge (Beverley). Below this point, landing is difficult due to the mud and the strong tidal current.

16½   Grovehill Lock and Beverley Beck. The Humber Keel Society floating exhibition is located here.

25   Hull Rowing Club, Hull University Rowing Club [TA 102314]. There are landing steps on the west bank.

27   There are no locks in the town section, but a tidal barrage is put into position to hold back high tides. Current on falling tide can be very rapid, allegedly 6 - 8 knots according to the boating clubs. There is much congestion with the moored barges and coasting vessels. It is NOT possible to land at low water below the rowing clubs due to deep mud. Landing is desperately difficult and even if a landing is effected canoeists may find themselves locked into a private dock area. It is better to proceed out into the estuary but this is only for the experienced paddlers. It can be rough, the tide will most likely be flowing out to sea and landing is still difficult due to the docks. Sammy's Point is known to have dangerous currents [TA 102282].

Tidal information: at Hull, low water is 8 hours after high water, hence the Ebb lasts for 8 hours and the Flood lasts for 41/2 hours. At Beverley, high water is 2 hours after high water at Hull. When British Summer Time is in force, do not forget to add 1 hour onto the Greenwich Mean Time (GMT) figure.

MARKET WEIGHTON CANAL

GRADE: 0

REMARKS: The canal is canoed regularly with a permit obtainable from the National Rivers Authority.

MAP REQUIRED: LANDRANGER 106.

ACCESS INFORMATION: There are no access agreements. The stretch of canal to the north of the River Foulness to Sodhouses Lock is closed to boats from April - June inclusive. There are many angling matches on Sundays.

LOCAL ACCESS OFFICER: Ted Smith
4 Wilton Terrace
HORNSEA HU18 1PX
(Tel 0964 534393)

GENERAL DESCRIPTION

A 6 mile long canal, originally intended to go from Market Weighton to the River Humber, now only extends to Sodhouses Lock. The main function of the canal is land drainage. Permits to use the canal can be obtained from the National Rivers Authority, free of charge, on application to the Divisional Office at Beverley. Access from the east bank near Newport is easy but parts of the west bank are sectioned for match fishing: most angling events take place on Sundays between 9 am and 3 pm. The canal is a useful stretch of water for training but not particularly interesting for cruising.

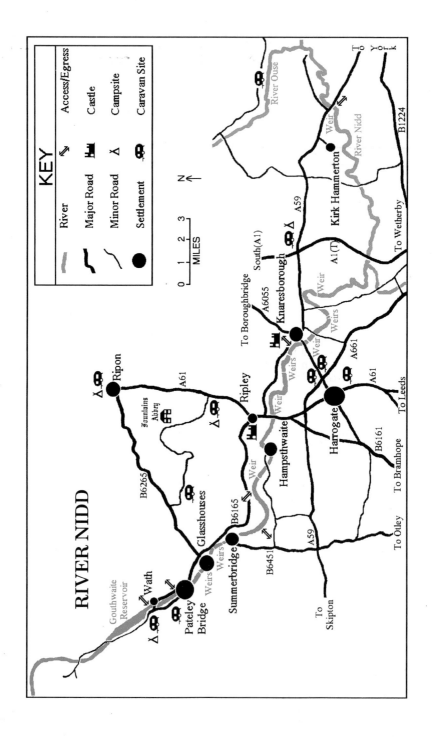

RIVER NIDD

GRADE:	I - II plus weirs.
REMARKS:	The Nidd is canoed regularly with no problems with anglers.
MAPS REQUIRED:	LANDRANGER 99,104 and 105.
ACCESS INFORMATION:	There are no access agreements.
LOCAL ACCESS OFFICER:	Chris Hawkesworth Glasshouses Mill Pateley Bridge HARROGATE HG3 5QH (Tel 0423 711624)

GENERAL DESCRIPTION

The River Nidd is a small shallow river with three reservoirs at the head of the valley. Two supply Bradford and the third, Gouthwaite, is a compensation reservoir. The river hardly rises above grade II all the way from Gouthwaite to its confluence with the Ouse at Nun Monkton. Due to the reservoirs it is only after heavy rain that there is much water in the river. Nidderdale is beautiful and unspoilt, and it is worth visiting such places as Brimham Rocks, Stump Cross Caverns and Howstean Gorge.

ITINERARY:

Miles

0   Wath Bridge [SE 144678]. Access at the bridge about 500 yards below Gouthwaite Reservoir.

1¾   Riverside Caravan and Campsite [SE 155658].

2   Pateley Bridge [SE 157655]. Access/egress can be made here.

2½   Bewerley Park Centre for Outdoor Pursuits.

2¾   Castlesteads Weir and Footbridge. Portage is possible on the left bank.

3   Glasshouses Road Bridge and Mill. There are 2 more weirs in the next 2½ miles. Beware of the spikes in the second weir. All of these can be dangerous in high water.

5¼   Summer Bridge Weir. Shoot the weir on the left or portage on the left bank.

5½   Summer Bridge.

7½   Darley [SE 205598]. Access/egress is possible here.

9   Ross Bridge [SE 230603]. A car park adjoins the river here and access/egress is possible 100 yards upstream of the bridge. Trips starting here usually avoid problems with anglers.

10   Birstwith Weir and Bridge. Portage is on the left bank.

11   Hampsthwaite Bridge.

13   Killinghall Bridge and Weir. This weir can be shot on the right through the slot or portaged on the right bank.

14¾   Nidd Railway Viaduct.

15½   Scotton Mill Weir. This weir should be shot in the centre or, if in doubt, portaged on the right bank.

17½   Small weir under footbridge. This is usually shootable in the centre.

18   Knaresborough [SE 345571]. Egress is possible on the left above the road bridge and parking is available in Conyngham Hall public car park. Hire craft use the next section of the river and they are not very keen on canoeists.

18¼ Railway viaduct.

18½ Castle Kirks Weir. This weir has been recently rebuilt. Portage is possible but difficult.

20   Grimbold Weirs and Road Bridge. From this point onwards, the river becomes very sluggish and is heavily fished.

21½ Goldsborough Mill Weir.

28   Walshford Bridge on the A1.

38   Skip Bridge on A59 [SE 483560]. There is a gauging weir here and access/egress can be made.

42   Nun Monkton [SE 513579]. The river now joins the Ouse.

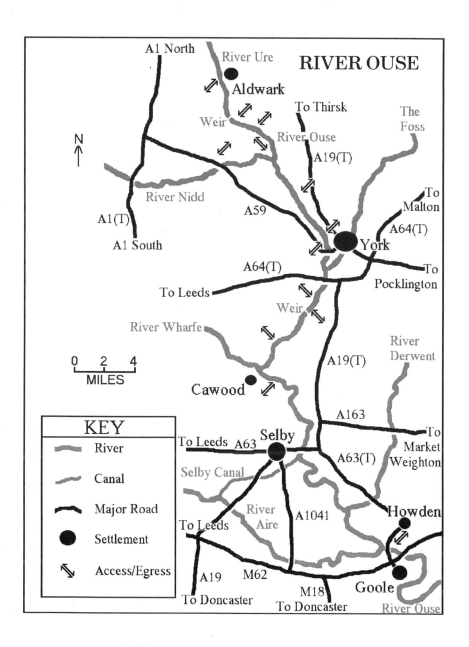

RIVER OUSE

RIVER OUSE

GRADE: 0 - I plus weirs.

REMARKS: The river is canoed regularly. The Ouse is a navigation in its entirety and tidal below Naburn Locks. Details of the navigation authorities involved in some stretches are given in the section on navigations and canals at the end of the guide.

MAPS REQUIRED: LANDRANGER 100, 105, 107, 112 and 113.

ACCESS INFORMATION: There are no access agreements.

LOCAL ACCESS OFFICER: Ron Rymer
The Lodge
Kirk Hammerton
YORK YO5 8BX
(Tel 0423 330323)

GENERAL DESCRIPTION

The River Ure changes its name just below Aldwark Bridge to become the River Ouse. The river then flows on through York and Selby and, at its junction with the River Trent, becomes the River Humber. Being a navigation for all of its length, the river is ideal for canoe touring with its long stretches of flat water. For the more experienced canoeists, however, the weir and fish ladder at Linton Locks can be a real challenge.

ITINERARY:

Miles

0   Aldwark Toll Bridge [SE 467622]. Access/egress is possible at the Scout's Watersports Centre.

1½   A large sign at Ure - Ouse boundary is on the right bank.

2   Linton Lock and Weir [SE 500602]. The channel to the lock is on the left hand side. The vertical weir is about 12 ft high and has a fish ladder on the right hand side. Access/egress can be made here. There is a campsite and cafe on the left bank.

3   Newton-on-Ouse [SE 510601]. Access/egress is possible from the public footpath, 100 yards on the left, downstream of the River Kyle.

4½   Nun Monkton [SE 513579]. An access/egress point is on the right hand side. The River Nidd joins the Ouse from the right.

8½   Nether Poppleton [SE 557552]. Access/egress is available on the right.

12   Clifton Landing [SE 580530]. Access/egress can be made at the public land on the left bank.

13   Clifton Bridge [SE 589528]. Access/egress is possible on the left hand side. Here, the many acres of public land may be suitable for camping and a YHA Youth Hostel is situated nearby.

15   York City Centre [SE 605518]. Access/egress is possible here. There are

many bridges crossing the river including the Scarborough Rail Bridge and Lendal, Ouse and Skeldergate Bridges.

15¼ Public Campsite on right hand bank [SE 604509].

16   York Ring Road bridge.

17   Bishopthorpe Palace [SE 597478]. This is the Archbishop of York's official residence. Access/egress is possible on the right hand bank just past the palace.

18   Naburn [SE 598455]. Access/egress at the public slipway.

18¼ Acaster Malbis [SE 592456]. Access/egress on the right hand side.

18¾ Naburn Locks and Weir [SE 594445]. Access/egress is possible on both sides of the river. The river is tidal below and, in flood conditions, above, the weir. If you are portaging, please be respectful to the lock-keeper and if you wish to launch from the east bank, ask his permission.

22   Acaster Selby [SE 575415]. Access/egress is possible on the right hand bank.

24   Confluence with the River Wharfe.

25   Cawood [SE 575379]. Access/egress at the Yorkshire Ouse Water Ski Club on the right hand bank, just before the bridge.

31   Selby. This section of the river has high muddy banks and a fast flowing tide which you should not try to paddle against. Selby toll bridge is dangerous since the fast flowing water piles rubbish up against its columns. This is a commercial navigation in which large barges and ships are also at the mercy of the tide. Selby Canal is on the right hand side.

38   Confluence with the River Derwent [SE 678287]. Access/egress can be made here. There is a tidal barrage across the Derwent.

39¾ Confluence with the River Aire.

40   Booth Ferry Bridge [SE 733263]. Access/egress is possible on the left hand side at the old ferry landing.

44   Hook [SE 763256]. Access/egress is possible but due to mud, this is not recommended at low water.

46   Goole Docks.

48¼ Swinfleet [SE 767220]. Again, access/egress is possible but due to mud, this is not recommended at low water.

51¼ Reedness [SE 799231]. Access/egress is possible but at low water it is not recommended because of the mud.

55½ Confluence with the River Trent. You are now on the River Humber. The main channel is on the right hand side but the left hand side is O.K.

62½ Read's Island [SE 9622]. Access/egress before the New River Ancholme is not recommended. You should be on the North Bank, the left hand side of the estuary, up to the Humber Bridge.

66½ Hessle Sands [TA 028253]. Access/egress is available at a shingle and sand beach. Eddies are present on this section of the estuary.

71   Hull Corporation Pier [TA 100281] . Access/egress can be made here.

76   Hull Corporation Harbour [TA 140285]. Access/egress is possible here.

94   Spurn Head [TA 395105]. Access/egress can be made here. Cleethorpes is on the right hand side but Bull Rock, in mid stream, may be worth a visit.

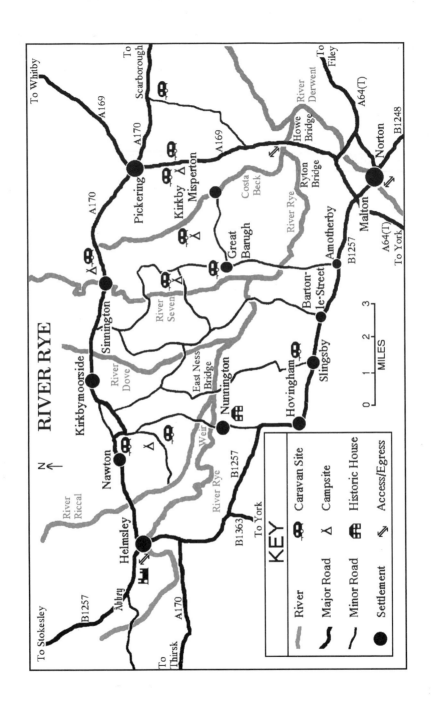

RIVER RYE

KEY

🚐 Caravan Site		
🛆 Campsite		
🏰 Historic House		
↗ Access/Egress		

River
Major Road
Minor Road
● Settlement

RIVER RYE

GRADE: I plus weirs.

REMARKS: The river is canoed quite regularly with no record of objection.

MAP REQUIRED: LANDRANGER 100.

ACCESS INFORMATION: There are no access agreements.

LOCAL ACCESS OFFICER: Neil Sanderson
8 Dean Road
Norton
MALTON YO17 9BX

GENERAL DESCRIPTION
The Rye rises in the Cleveland Hills and flows south-east between the Mableton and the Tabular Hills, past Rievaulx Abbey and Helmsley to meet the Derwent at Marishes where it is carrying twice as much water than the River Derwent.

ITINERARY
Miles
0   Helmsley [SE 615836].
6½   Nunnington Weir [SE 672795].
7½   East Ness Bridge [SE 688793].
16½   Ryton Bridge [SE 796754].
17½   Howe Bridge [SE 809760]. This is a good access/egress point.
19   Confluence with the Derwent [SE 825757].

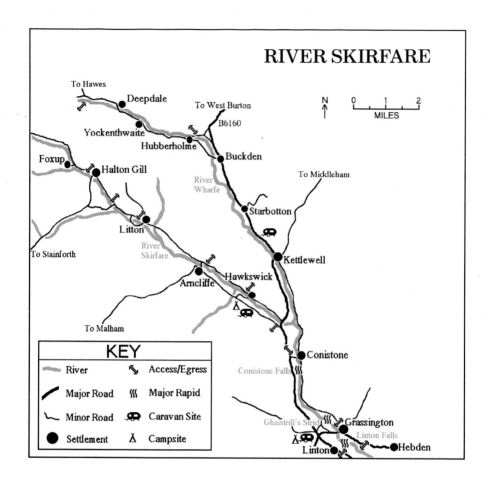

RIVER SKIRFARE

KEY

River	Access/Egress
Major Road	Major Rapid
Minor Road	Caravan Site
Settlement	Campsite

RIVER SKIRFARE

GRADE:	III - IV above Arncliffe. II below Arncliffe.
REMARKS:	This seldomly canoed river is only possible in high water.
MAP REQUIRED:	LANDRANGER 98.
ACCESS INFORMATION:	There are no access agreements.
LOCAL ACCESS OFFICER:	Mike Twiggs 38 Badger Gate Threshfield SKIPTON BD23 5EN (Tel 0756 753101)

GENERAL DESCRIPTION

The river above Arncliffe is only canoeable in very high water, when it is a good grade III - IV, although extra care should be taken on this section as there are a number of wire boundary fences across the river. Below Arncliffe, the river calms down with some grade II rapids leading to Ammerdale Dub, the confluence with the River Wharfe.

ITINERARY

Miles

0   Halton Gill [SD 880763]. Access is possible at the road bridge where there is room to park.

2   Stainforth Old Road [SD 899742]. Access and parking is available just above the bridge.

2½   Litton. There is a footpath to the river here. In high water, a stopper forms below the ford to East Garth Farm but it is easy to portage this on the left bank.

3   Below Litton there is a large rock island in the centre of the river and inspection is advised. A footpath runs along the right hand side of the river, to within 1 mile of Arncliffe.

4½   Arncliffe [SD 934720]. Access/egress is possible just below the village on the left hand side of the river near the Hawkswick Road, but there is only room for 3 or 4 cars.

6   Hawkswick [SD 956705]. Access/egress can be made above the road bridge on either side of the river.

7½   Kettlewell Road [SD 972692]. Access/egress is available above the bridge.

8   Ammerdale Dub [SD 978693]. This is the confluence with the River Wharfe.

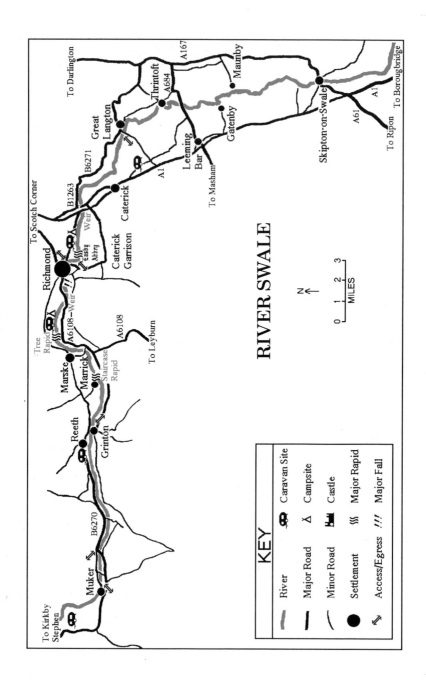

RIVER SWALE

N

0 1 2 3
MILES

KEY

River   Caravan Site

Major Road   Campsite

Minor Road   Castle

Settlement   Major Rapid

Access/Egress   Major Fall

RIVER SWALE

GRADE: II - III.

REMARKS: The river is canoed regularly. A good introduction to the Swale is provided by the annual Swale Charity Paddle between Grinton and Brompton-on-Swale. The river is a navigation below Morton Bridge.

MAPS REQUIRED: LANDRANGER 92, 98 and 99.

ACCESS INFORMATION: There is one access agreement. The Local Access Officer should be contacted for details before any trip on the river is planned.

LOCAL ACCESS OFFICER: Lofty Wright
2 Scotton Road
Catterick Garrison
CATTERICK DL9 3PG

GENERAL DESCRIPTION

Rising above Keld on Birkdale Common, the River Swale flows east to Richmond, then swings gradually south until its confluence with the River Ure at Swale Nab, near Boroughbridge. In high water much of the Swale above Catterick is grade III but in dry weather it is rather shallow due to the almost continuous fall to Catterick. However, the river rises swiftly after heavy or prolonged rain or melting snowfall to provide the chance of an exciting canoe trip.

ITINERARY

Miles

0   Muker [SD 911978]. In order to access the river, it is necessary to launch onto Muker Beck and then paddle the 50 yards down to the Swale.

½   Large pebble banks. The channel is to be found on the left hand side.

1   Bend and small island with the channel on the left hand side. This is followed by rapids strewn with numerous rocks.

1½   A stream enters on the right, followed by a bridge with many rocks below. This section has a channel to the left, followed by several small rapids and then a pebble bank and a channel on the right hand side.

3   Gunnerside Bridge [SD 950978]. Take the left arch of the bridge. Gunnerside Gill enters on the left and then 100 yards further on is a small island. There is a good access/egress point on the left but there are also several easy access points before Grinton Bridge.

9   Grinton Bridge [SE 047985]. Access is possible from the left bank below the bridge.

10   Marrick Priory. The Staircase Rapid is followed by a right hand bend and rocky rapids.

13½   Rocky rapids leading to Marske Road Bridge. Take the channel on the right, past two islands.

14¼   Marske Beck enters here, followed by deeper water.

15   Left hand bend. A distinct channel on the right hand side peters out and a rapid paddle, crossing over to the left, is needed to avoid the shallows. This is followed by a heavy rapid which sweeps into a submerged tree. Care should be taken since a number of canoes have been written off here in recent years.

16   Swale View Camping and Caravan site [NZ 134014].

17   Lowenthwaite Bridge and Pumping Station. Very sharp rocks lie just below the surface under the bridge, followed by strong rotary currents. Following this, there is a left hand bend with slabs and large rocks. The water is flowing very fast by the District Council caravan site, which is on the left bank.

18½   Right hand bend and weir. Here, there is very confused water and a high wall on the left. The next 100 yards are studded with rocks as the channel swings from left to right, ending in a deep pool on a bend. There is a fine view of Richmond Castle standing sentinel above the river.

19   Richmond Town Fall [NZ 173006]. This 8 ft sheer drop can be shot, but a special safety code must be observed. Contact the Local Access Officer concerning this. Portage the fall on the left, then launch left of the island below the rocks.

19½   Station Bridge. Shallow rapids, with a channel on the right, are followed by deeper water. The banks on this stretch are tree lined.

20½   Broken weir [NZ 185003]. This should be shot straight forward. The weir is followed by a car park on the left bank and you can access/egress here, but only from the bend below the car park, along a private road/public footpath.

21   Easby Slalom Site. There are rapids and an island. The channel is on the left and then on the right up to the railway bridge.

21½   Red House Farm. A confused rapid is followed by a still and deep stretch of water.

22½   Broken Brae. A right hand bend is followed by an island, the channel here is to the left.

23   Brompton-on-Swale. There is a lay-by on the left hand side. A right and then a left hand bend are followed by a confused rapid where the channel is in the centre.

23¾   Catterick Bridge. Old Great North Road. Take the right hand arch. A stopper is caused by a small weir under the bridge which is followed by a small island. From there to Great Langton there are numerous gravel banks, small rapids and trees causing obstructions. This section has a wilderness character and is ideal for Canadian Canoeing.

30   Great Langton Bridge [SE 290965]. Access/egress can be made through the wood by the Village War Memorial. From here the river is slow and it meanders between high banks. It is all of 40 miles to Swale Nab.

40   Morton Bridge [SE 319918].

52   Skipton-on-Swale.

54   Catton.

57   Topcliffe Bridge [SE 398760].

63½   Thornton Bridge [SE 433715].

64½   Brafferton Railway Bridge [SE 434704].

65   Brafferton.

68   Myton-on-Swale.

69   Swale Nab [SE 431660]. The confluence with the River Ure.

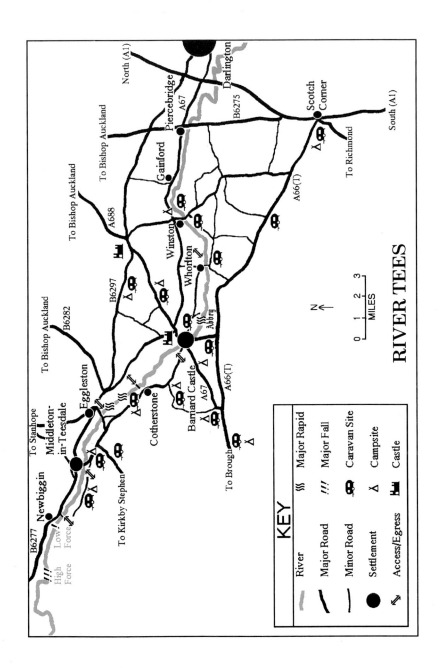

KEY

River	〜	Major Rapid	〰
Major Road	\	Major Fall	!!!
Minor Road	)	Caravan Site	⚏
Settlement	●	Campsite	Δ
Access/Egress	⤡	Castle	⌂

RIVER TEES

N ↙

0 1 2 3
MILES

RIVER TEES

GRADE:	III - IV.
REMARKS:	The river is canoed regularly by agreement.
MAPS REQUIRED:	LANDRANGER 92 and 93.
ACCESS INFORMATION:	There are access agreements on the High Force to Winston sections of the river. These allow canoeing on certain days during November to March inclusive and on more limited stretches of water at some other times of the year. The Local Access Officer organises the management of the access and must be consulted for details of the dates etc on which these sections are open. All terms of agreements must be strictly adhered to otherwise the future of the access agreement may be jeopardised.
LOCAL ACCESS OFFICER:	Len Smith Four Seasons Adventure Store 44 The Bank BARNARD CASTLE DL12 8PN (Tel 0833 37829)

GENERAL DESCRIPTION

The Tees rises on Cross Fell and from Caldron Snout to the sea, it forms the boundary between Yorkshire and Durham. In its upper reaches, from High Force to well below Barnard Castle, it is still very much a white water canoeist's river and several stretches are extremely difficult. The above sections of the river rise rapidly after rain and should always demand respect. Downstream of Winston the river is much quieter, passing through industrial Teeside, but the river mouth itself has much to offer to enterprising sea canoeists.

ANALYSIS

Fall is given in feet per mile (fpm)

SECTION	FALL(fpm)	GRADING	CONDITIONS
High Force to Wynch Bridge	75-100	III - IV	Best in high water.
Wynch Bridge to Eggleston	30	III	Best in high water.
Eggleston to Cotherstone	40	III - IV	Best in high water. Do not tackle lightly.

Cotherstone to Abbey Rapids	20	III - IV	Canoeable in medium water.
Abbey Rapids to Winston	25	III	Canoeable in medium water.
Winston to Middlesbrough	10	I	This is feasible at most levels.

ITINERARY
Miles

0   High Force [NY 881284]. Access to below the falls can be made via the path from the High Force Hotel although a fee may be charged. During the next 1 mile, there are numerous grade II - III rapids.

1   Grade III - IV rapids.

1½   Low Force. This 15 ft waterfall should only be attempted by the expert paddler, only in acceptable conditions and with adequate support. If in doubt, portage on the right bank. Immediately following this, is a grade III-IV fall.

1¾   Wynch Bridge lies just below Low Force [NY 904279]. To access/egress here, carry boats along the footpath from the B6277. The middle section towards Middleton contains 3 weirs which, in high water, should be viewed with caution and portaged on the right bank if in doubt.

3½   Middleton Bridge [NY 947252]. Launch from the right bank by the gate near to some shingle.

4¾   Grade III rapids. The confluence with the River Lune is on the right.

7   Eggleston Bridge [NY 997233]. The Tees Wild Water Race starts here and it is also a popular slalom venue. Launch upstream of the bridge on the right bank.

7½   Beginning of the gorge section termed 'The Racecourse'. Difficult falls and rapids follow one another in quick succession. One rapid, with many boulders where the river disappears around a bend, may need to be inspected beforehand from the left bank.

8   Woden Croft. The rapids now become easier.

9   Cotherstone Iron Bridge [NZ 014203]. The river opens out here at the finish of the Wild Water Race course. Egress on the left bank.

11½   Beware of the sudden steep fall at the end of a heavy rapid.

12   Railway bridge.

13   Barnard Castle Footbridge [NZ 046167]. This is a good egress point with the main road on the right hand side. Warren's Dam, recently rebuilt, is dangerous to shoot in the centre due to a vicious stopper. Shoot either side or portage on the left.

13½   Barnard Castle Town Bridge. Broken weirs and ledges are to be found in this section.

14   Lendings Mill Campsite and Caravan park (address: Startforth, Barnard Castle) [NZ 154156].

14¾   Egglestone Abbey on the right. This should not to be confused with Eggleston, 8 miles upstream.

15½   Abbey Rapids (grade IV) and Abbey Bridge. The falls in which the Abbey Rapids culminate are much worse than they look from the road. Rescue can be difficult in high water conditions. The River Greta enters from the left after the rapids.

19   Whorlton Bridge.

19½   Whorlton Falls [NZ 114145]. These must be inspected first. Rescue is difficult in the middle section in high water. Portage is possible on either bank but is perhaps easier on the right. A car park nearby is useful for access/egress. The next section includes many ledges which change the river character according to water level, building large stoppers in high water.

21½   Winston Reefs followed by Winston Bridge [NZ 142163]. Access/egress on the left bank above the bridge.

27½   Piercebridge. The river is very shallow from here to Croft.

39½   Croft [NZ 290098]. Access/egress is possible on the right hand side below the bridge.

41½   Dalton Island. In flood conditions the right hand channel can be dangerous due to the footbridge support cables, and trees are a danger in the left channel.

42¾   Hurworth [NZ 311101]. Access/egress on the right at the bridge.

44½   Neasham [NZ 327103]. An access/egress point is on the left. Weeds occur for about 1 mile.

52½   Dinsdale [NZ 346114]. In high water, there are good rapids above the bridge. Access/egress is possible on the left hand side below the bridge. From here the river is very extensively used for fishing matches, almost every Sunday, and these matches can often involve over 100 contestants.

54   Middleton-One-Row [NZ 350124]. Access/egress on the left, up the steep bank to the road. The effect of the tide can be felt some distance downstream of here. The banks can become rather muddy, but the river is still interesting with a varied wildlife. There are many ducks of various kinds during the season.

55½   Low Middleton Hall [NZ 363106]. There is a new weir with sharp metal sill. A camp site is situated 200 yards upstream above the round tower on the left. The Rowing Club steps lie 200 yards after the second bridge.

62½   Yarm [NZ 415122]. Access/egress on the right. The river is definitely tidal here.

63   There is a grade II rapid at low tide which is good for practice. The stretch from here to Stockton is the Hartlepool LD Racecourse. The river is deep and fast flowing, but one has to plan according to the tide.

71½   Thornaby. This marks the start of industrial Teeside.

74½   Norton Bridge.

78   Middlesborough Transporter Bridge.

82   Seal Sands on the left [NZ 540264]. There is a channel to the right. On sunny days seals may be basking here and many ships may be seen alongside the jetties or the floating pipelines. The sands are firm and a landing may be made at low tide. At high tide there is also a great concentration of bird life, as the Seal Sands are a natural stop-over point for Arctic migrants heading south and other migrants heading north. As a result, the wildlife is varied and of national interest.

84   Redcar Jetty [NZ 548265]. Across from this it is possible to paddle up the channel on the north side of Seal Sands.

86½   South Gare Breakwater and Lighthouse [NZ 558284]. Tees Mouth. DO NOT proceed on the ebb tide since it is very exposed and risky situations may arise.

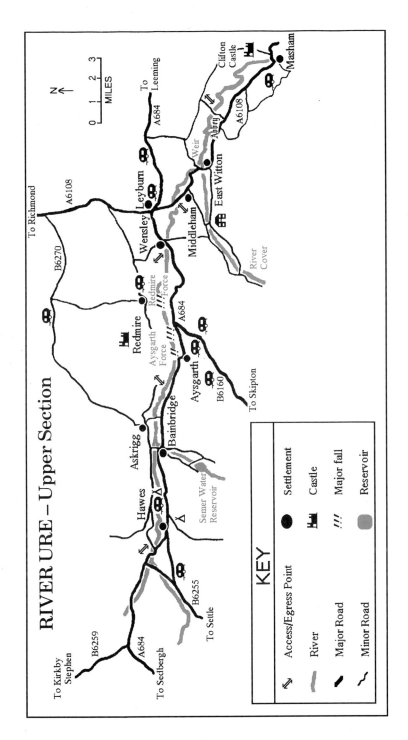

RIVER URE – Upper Section

KEY

Access/Egress Point
River
Major Road
Minor Road

Settlement
Castle
Major fall
Reservoir

N

0 1 2 3
MILES

To Richmond
A6108
B6270
To Kirkby Stephen
B6259
A684
To Sedbergh
B6255
To Settle
Hawes
Askrigg
Bainbridge
Semer Water Reservoir
Redmire
Redmire Force
Aysgarth Force
Aysgarth
B6160
To Skipton
Wensley
Leyburn
Middleham
East Witton
River Cover
Weir
Aldbrough
A684
A6108
Clifton Castle
Masham
To Leeming

RIVER URE

GENERAL DESCRIPTION
The River Ure is the most canoeable of the Yorkshire Pennine rivers, in that it carries more water than any of the others. It is particularly suitable for novices, canoe campers, and others who favour long, trouble-free stretches and for expedition work. Middleham Bridge is one of the best starting points. The famous Hack Falls, between Masham and West Tanfield is downstream of here and, though exciting, does not require advanced paddling techniques. The most difficult stretch of the river is between Aysgarth Force and Wensley. This has several heavy rapids, and one set of falls- Redmire Force. You will probably need to portage past most of Aysgarth Force.

Source to Masham

GRADE: I - III.

REMARKS: The river is canoed by agreement. Masham village is not very friendly towards canoeists and has threatened legal action.

MAPS REQUIRED: LANDRANGER 98 and 99.

ACCESS INFORMATION: There are access agreements on some sections of the river. You must contact the Local Access Officer for details before planning any trip.

LOCAL ACCESS OFFICER: Colin Stegeman
17 Quarry Road
RICHMOND DL10 4BP
(Tel 0748 823861)

ANALYSIS
Fall is given in feet per mile (fpm)

SECTION	FALL(fpm)	GRADING	REMARKS
Hawes to Aysgarth	15	I - II	Best in medium and high water.
Aysgarth Force	–	–	Impossible in any water conditions.
Aysgarth to Bolton Bridge	30	III	This can be grade V in flood.
Bolton Bridge to Masham	10	I - II	Canoeable at most levels.

ITINERARY

Miles

0   Hawes [SD 877904]. Launch at the bridge on the road to Hardraw.

4   Yorebridge. Bainbridge is immediately on the right and Grange and Askrigg on the left. The River Bain entering below the bridge leads from Semer Water Reservoir.

8¾   Metal footbridge [SD 996889]. This is the best disembarking place for portaging Aysgarth Force.

9¼   Aysgarth Force [SE 003888]. This is impossible to canoe.

10   Aysgarth Bridge [SE 011886]. Cars may be parked here in the public car park and boats portaged along the footpath which follows the north bank of the river. Launch below the Middle Falls, ferry glide across the river and portage the Lower Falls along the south bank. Small parties may park on the main A684 road and portage less than 200 yards along a track to the foot of the Lower Falls.

12¼   Redmire Force [SE 045901]. Portage on the left bank.

12½   Footpath to Redmire village. The next 2 miles of the river contain many excellent Grade III rapids.

14½   Bolton Hall Bridge (private).

15½   Wensley Bridge [SE 092895]. Access/egress can be made here.

18   Middleham Bridge [SE 119888]. This is a popular starting point.

18½   Middleham Busks.

21   Ulshaw Bridge and Weir. The weir is usually shootable.

23½   Jervaulx Abbey [SE 166860].

26   Kilgram Grange Bridge and egress point [SE 192860].

31   Clifton Castle. Squirrel Banks Rapid.

33   Masham Bridge [SE 226813].

Masham to Sleningford Watermill

GRADE: II - III.

REMARKS: Some sections are canoed regularly by agreement. There is severe harassment by anglers outside agreed waters near Masham. Masham village is not very friendly towards canoeists and has threatened legal action.

MAP REQUIRED: LANDRANGER 99.

ACCESS INFORMATION: Access agreements are in force at Mickley and Sleningford Watermill. The conditions of these must be strictly adhered to. Ask for details from the Local Access Officer or at Sleningford Watermill (Tel 0765 635201).

Access is normally gained via the public footpath through the wood some 300 yards north-west of Mickley village. Please leave vehicles at Sleningford where possible and not at Mickley. At Sleningford Caravan Park please inform Francis Petchey, the site manager, and pay the car park fee. Paddlers can also use the site itself with the adjoining rapids for canoeing.

LOCAL ACCESS OFFICER: Ken Harrap
159 Old Road
Overton
WAKEFIELD WF4 4RR
(Tel 0924 274843(H) / 0532 442066(W))

ANALYSIS
Fall is given in feet per mile (fpm)

SECTION	FALL(fpm)	GRADING	REMARKS
Masham to Sleningford	15	II - III	Canoeable in medium and high water.

ITINERARY
Miles
33   Masham [SE 226813]. As noted above this is not a very good place to start or finish.
36   Hack Falls. These consist of a very large and frightening rapid on a double bend in the river. However the pool at the bottom provides some security for

46

those that swim. The rapid should be shot on the left hand side of the river. There are a number of breakouts on both sides of the main channel and a large rock in the centre which may be covered in high water. The falls should be portaged or inspected from the right bank.

37   Mickley Weir [SE 253771]. This was modified in 1967 when a small turbine and a salmon trap were installed. Shoot on the left hand side since the weir is very steep on the right. Access/egress is possible on the right bank above and below the weir.

37/40 A number of rocky rapids provide a classic exercise in rock dodging. In high water there are good standing waves.

40   West Tanfield Bridge. Access/egress is not possible here.

40½   Tanfield Weir. This MUST be shot on the right hand side or portaged on the right bank. The river then cuts a shallow gorge in the Permian strata with lots of breakouts, standing waves and pools to play in.

41   Sleningford Watermill Caravan Park and Campsite [SE 280784]. These rapids are the scene of much canoeing activity, including a Division 4/5 Slalom held in September. There is a shop on the site with canoeing gear and refreshments for sale.

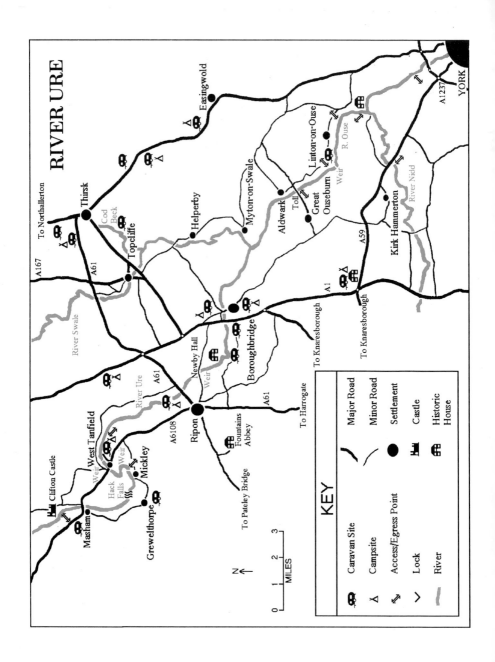

Sleningford to the Ouse

GRADE: I - II.

REMARKS: The river is a navigation below Ox Close Lock and, at the confluence with Ouse Gill Beck, becomes the River Ouse.

MAPS REQUIRED: LANDRANGER 99 and 100.

ACCESS INFORMATION: There are no access agreements.

LOCAL ACCESS OFFICER: Ken Harrap
159 Old Road
Overton
WAKEFIELD WF4 4RR
(Tel 0924 274843(H) / 0532 442066(W))

ANALYSIS
Fall is given in feet per mile (fpm)

SECTION	FALL(fpm)	GRADING	REMARKS
Sleningford to the Ouse	10	I - II	Canoeable at most levels.

ITINERARY

Miles
42   Batts Nature Reserve [SE 293776].
46   Ripon Bridge. Beware of waves under the bridge in high water.
47½ Bridge Hewick. There is a small weir under the bridge.
49   Ox Close Lock, Ripon Canal. The River Ure is now a navigation.
50½ Bishop Monkton. Army bridging site which may be used for parking if prior permission is obtained.
50¾ Newby Hall [SE 345674].
51½ Westwick Weir. Weir Island and Westwick lock.
55   Boroughbridge. There is a weir and a lock as well as sailing clubs.
57¼ Confluence with the River Swale.
60¾ Aldwark Bridge [SE 467622]. The Scout's Watersports Centre lies just downstream.
62   Confluence with Ouse Gill Beck [SE 474602]. The river is now called the Ouse.

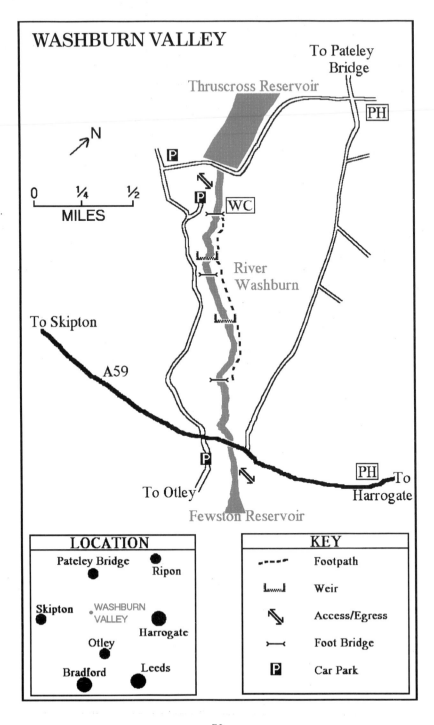

WASHBURN VALLEY

To Pateley Bridge

Thruscross Reservoir

PH

N

0   ¼   ½
MILES

P

P

WC

River Washburn

To Skipton

A59

To Otley

P

PH To Harrogate

Fewston Reservoir

LOCATION

Pateley Bridge
Ripon
Skipton
WASHBURN VALLEY
Harrogate
Otley
Bradford
Leeds

KEY

- - - - Footpath

Weir

Access/Egress

Foot Bridge

P Car Park

50

RIVER WASHBURN

GRADE:	III.
REMARKS:	The river is a very popular venue during water releases for both recreational and competitive canoeing.
MAP REQUIRED:	LANDRANGER 104.
ACCESS INFORMATION:	During water releases, canoeists have access/egress at numerous places along the river. During cruises, it is normal to launch by the car park at the beginning of the course [SE 155574] and egress near the car park adjacent to the A59 Harrogate to Skipton road [SE 169554].

GENERAL DESCRIPTION

The River Washburn, a tributary of the Wharfe, and the four large reservoirs of the Washburn Valley provide the main water supply catchment area for Leeds. Except during water releases, the river joining the reservoirs is normally dry and canoeing impossible. Paddling on the reservoirs and above is strictly prohibited. On about 20 days in the year water releases for canoeing purposes are made from 'Thruscross' into 'Fewston' Reservoirs. Events at Washburn currently include Wednesday evening and weekend cruises and slalom and wild water racing- the contacts below will supply full details.

The 1½ miles of grade III fast flowing water between the two reservoirs has become the most important and heavily used competition site in England. Used mainly for slalom and wild water races, it is also open for touring paddlers. The river has three slalom sites, one of which is used for each slalom competition.

On river race days the river can be cruise paddled by non-racing paddlers by prior arrangement with the event organiser. It can be a most exciting trip. When only one slalom site is in use, each of the other two are available for competitive or recreational use by prior arrangement with the Access Officer. The lower site near the A57 Harrogate to Skipton road is Division 4/5 standard. The other two sites are Premier to Division 3 standard. Active participation by clubs is encouraged by the Washburn Committee.

For availability and charges contact Don Player.

The site owners- Yorkshire Water P.L.C.- have vested all canoeing operations in the Washburn Committee of the Regional BCU. The Washburn Committee manages the river on behalf of all canoeists. A small fee is charged for parking at all events and for use of the river by non-competitive entrants. All paddlers must be members of the BCU or a BCU-affiliated club. Further information can be obtained from either the Wild Water Racing or Slalom Year Books or from:

Don Player – Dates/allocation of use – Access Officer.
21 The Drive, Roundhay, LEEDS LS8 1JF.
(Tel 0532 667397)

Chris Hawkesworth – Chairman.
The Mill, Glasshouses, Pateley Bridge, HARROGATE HG3 5QH.
(Tel 0423 711624(W) / 0423 711819(H))

Peter Grove – Treasurer.
Greystones, Queens Drive, ILKLEY LS29 9QW.
(Tel 0943 600944)

Hugh Pashley – Hon. Secretary.
10 Crawshaw Grove, SHEFFIELD S8 7EB.
(Tel 0742 747874)

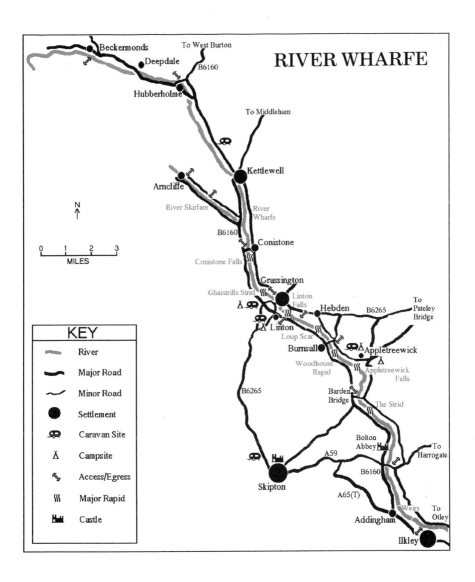

RIVER WHARFE

Beckermonds
Deepdale
To West Burton
B6160
Hubberholme
To Middleham

Kettlewell
Arncliffe
River Skirfare
River Wharfe
B6160
Conistone
Conistone Falls

Grassington
Ghaistrills Strid
Linton Falls
Hebden
B6265
To Pateley Bridge
Linton
Loup Scar
Burnsall
Appletreewick
Woodhouse Rapid
Appletreewick Falls
B6265
Barden Bridge
The Strid

Bolton Abbey
A59
To Harrogate

Skipton
B6160
A65(T)
Weirs
To Otley
Addingham
Ilkley

N

| 0 | 1 | 2 | 3 |
MILES

KEY

〰	River
∿	Major Road
⌒	Minor Road
●	Settlement
🚐	Caravan Site
Ⅹ	Campsite
↘	Access/Egress
⦓	Major Rapid
⛫	Castle

RIVER WHARFE

GENERAL DESCRIPTION

The River Wharfe is one of the best white water rivers in Yorkshire. Its proximity to the large towns of Leeds and Bradford makes it doubly valuable to a large number of canoeists.

Source to Linton Falls

GRADE: III - IV in high water.

REMARKS: The river is canoed regularly with no record of objection.

MAP REQUIRED: LANDRANGER 98.

ACCESS INFORMATION: There are no access agreements.

LOCAL ACCESS OFFICER: Mike Twiggs
38 Badger Gate
Threshfield
SKIPTON BD23 5EN
(Tel 0756 753101)

ANALYSIS
Fall is given in feet per mile (fpm)

SECTION	FALL(fpm)	GRADING	REMARKS
Beckermonds to Hubberholme	50	III - IV	Canoeable in high water only.
Hubberholme to Hebden	20	III	Canoeable at high water only.

ITINERARY
Miles

0   Beckermonds [SD 875803]. Launch at the footbridge on the road to Low Green Field. The river enters a short gorge with a series of falls up to 5 feet high. The road rejoins and follows the river. There are continuous rapids with small falls, below which stoppers form in high water.

2¼   Yockenthwaite Bridge. The river parts from the road at this point and enters a gorge section with rapids. There is a wire fence across the river.

4   Hubberholme Bridge. There is very little fall on this section but trees and fences crossing the river present a hazard.

9   Kettlewell. There is a car park next to the river. This series of rapids is best in medium water. Trees can be a problem along this section.

11   Ammerdale Dub, confluence with the River Skirfare [SD 978693]. Access is

possible ½ mile up the Skirfare at the road bridge.

11¾ Conistone Bridge [SD 979675]. Access/egress is possible here.

12½ Mill Scar Lash Falls (Conistone Falls). This rocky cataract, which falls in two steps, can be shot on the right in high water or portaged on the right bank.

14½ Ghaistrills Strid. Inspect this from the left bank. The strid is dangerous in low water. In medium water, go down the left side of the island and then cross to the right hand side. In high water the strid can be shot on both sides.

15 Grassington Bridge [SD 998639]. Access and egress is possible here.

15½ Linton Mill Weir. This can be shot on the right (down the side of the old turbine house) in low or medium water, but the weir is dangerous in high water.

15¾ Linton Falls [SE 002634]. The falls are canoeable, but should be inspected first. Portage is possible on the left bank. This is the usual finishing point for Upper Wharfe trips and there is a large car park at Linton Falls.

Linton to Barden Bridge

GRADE: III - IV.

REMARKS: Certain sections are canoed regularly by agreement.

MAPS REQUIRED: LANDRANGER 98 and 104.

ACCESS INFORMATION: There is an access agreement which permits the Burnsall to Barden sections to be canoed on about fourteen specific weekend days during the period October through to March. The Local Access Officer must be contacted if there is any doubt concerning the days, times etc. when this stretch of river is open for canoeing. Appletreewick Falls is open in addition to the above on the first Wednesday of each month except August from 12 noon. Use outside the periods specified will jeopardise the future of the agreements.

LOCAL ACCESS OFFICER: Don Player
                              21 The Drive
                              Roundhay
                              LEEDS LS8 1JF
                              (Tel 0532 667397)

ANALYSIS
Fall is given in feet per mile (fpm)

SECTION	FALL(fpm)	GRADING	REMARKS
Hebden to Barden	27	III - IV	This is best in high water.

ITINERARY
Miles

16¼ Linton Stepping Stones [SE 007631]. The next ½ mile consists of flat water.

17½ Hebden Footbridge [SE 025624]. Take the road from Burnsall to Hebden. There is room to park at the roadside and access is possible at the side of the suspension bridge.

18 Loup Scar. This is very exciting in high water, with lots of eddies and pools at the bottom for swimmers.

18½ Burnsall Bridge [SE 033612]. This is an access/egress point with a large car park and is the starting place of the Wharfe Wild Water Race.

19 Woodhouse Rapid. This should be shot by starting off on the left and then crossing over to the right for the last section. A large rock in the centre provides good standing waves in high water. There is a pool at the bottom.

56

20½ Appletreewick Falls. Inspection is possible from the left or right bank. The Top Fall should be shot on the right, entering the pool on the right. The stopper will pull you back if shot in the centre. The Bottom Fall has large standing waves at the bottom in high water but ends in a pool for any swimmers. In very high water this section can be dangerous. The falls are the site of a Division 2 Slalom event.

22   Barden Bridge [SE 053574]. Egress on the left hand bank, above the bridge. Parking is possible.

END OF SECTION COVERED BY AGREEMENT

Barden Bridge to Bolton Bridge

GRADE:	III - V.
REMARKS:	This section is canoed regularly by agreement.
MAP REQUIRED:	LANDRANGER 104.
ACCESS INFORMATION:	For details of the access agreement, contact the Local Access Officer or The Estate Office, Bolton Abbey Estate (Tel 0756 710227). The conditions of the agreement must be respected.
LOCAL ACCESS OFFICER:	John Morgan 77 St Richards Road OTLEY LS21 2AL (Tel 0943 464826)

ANALYSIS
Fall is given in feet per mile (fpm)

SECTION	FALL(fpm)	GRADING	REMARKS
Barden to Bolton Abbey	35	III - V	Prior inspection is always essential.

ITINERARY
Miles
22   Barden Bridge [SE 053574]. There is a car park here and access is from the left bank.
22¾ Tankers Corner. The heavy rapid gives very little opportunity in high water to break out before the Little Strid. Inspect and portage if in any doubt. Anyone capsizing here is in danger of being swept down through the Strid.
23   The Strid [SE 064566]. Only canoeable in high water- the Strid is very dangerous.
24½ Cavendish Pavilion Teahouse [SE 078553]. There is a footbridge and car park.
25½ Bolton Priory [SE 075543]. This is the site of a footbridge, stepping stones, and ledges.
26   Bolton Bridge [SE 072529]. Egress is possible on the right bank. A59 Harrogate/Skipton road.

Bolton Bridge to Otley

GRADE: I - II plus weirs.

REMARKS: This section is canoed regularly.

MAP REQUIRED: LANDRANGER 104.

ACCESS INFORMATION: There are no access agreements.

LOCAL ACCESS OFFICER: John Morgan
77 St Richards Road
OTLEY LS21 2AL
(Tel 0943 464826)

ANALYSIS
Fall is given in feet per mile (fpm)

SECTION	FALL(fpm)	GRADING	REMARKS
Bolton Bridge to Addingham	15	II	Canoeable in medium water.
Addingham to Otley	7	I	Canoeable in medium water.

ITINERARY
Miles
27   Lobwood Pumping Station and Weir [SE 076519]. The water which is released from Grimwith Reservoir is pumped out of the river at this point. The weir should be inspected and can be shot at the centre slot.
27½ Addingham Suspension Bridge.
28   Addingham High Weir. This can be shot on the left but should be inspected first.
29   Addingham Low Weir. This stepped weir can be portaged on the left bank.
30   Ilkley [SE 113482]. Access/egress is possible here.
32½ Ben Rhydding Bridge [SE 138482]. An access/egress point is situated here.
35½ Burley-in-Wharfedale. The weir can be portaged on the left bank.
39   Otley Weir [SE 203460]. This weir can be portaged on the left bank.

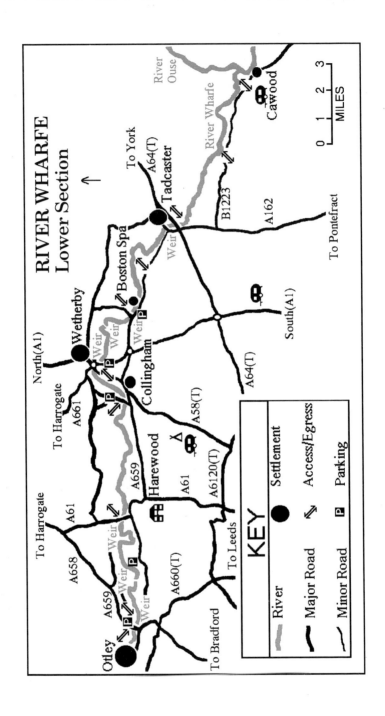

RIVER WHARFE
Lower Section

KEY

Settlement

Access/Egress

Parking

River

Major Road

Minor Road

Otley to Cawood

GRADE: I.

REMARKS: This section is canoed regularly. The river is tidal below Tadcaster.

MAPS REQUIRED: LANDRANGER 104 and 105.

ACCESS INFORMATION: There are no access agreements.

LOCAL ACCESS OFFICER: Peter Arter
4 Wetherby Road
TADCASTER LS24 9JN
(Tel 0937 833876)

ANALYSIS
Fall is given in feet per mile (fpm)

SECTION	FALL(fpm)	GRADING	REMARKS
Otley to Collingham	7	I	Canoeable at most water levels.
Collingham to Tadcaster	3	I	Canoeable at most water levels.

ITINERARY
Miles
39 Otley Weir [SE 203461].
40½ Knotford Nook Gravel Pit.
41 Pool Paper Mill Weir. This is canoeable but can be portaged on the left bank.
41¾ Pool-in-Wharfedale Bridge [SE 244455]. Access/egress is possible below the bridge on the left bank.
42½ Castley/Riffa Beck [SE 257458]. Turn first right after Pool Bridge. There is ample parking where the road meets the river.
43 Arthington Viaduct [SE 264455]. Good access is available along Warren Lane and parking is available under the viaduct. This should be shot through the left or middle arch, but beware of trees on the left bank in high water.
48½ Harewood Upper Weir. This is canoeable but can be portaged on the left bank.
49 Harewood Road Bridge [SE 312461]. If the steps under the bridge cannot be shot, egress on the left bank at the other side of the bridge. Access to the river is then possible on the right hand side.
50¾ Netherby [SE 330467]. Access/egress is possible on the left bank. There is a track from the river to the road, with parking available on the public road.
53¼ Iron Footbridge, Ox Close Wood. There is a public footpath from East Keswick Lane End, where cars must be parked.
55 Collingham [SE 389465]. There is an access/egress point on the right hand side past the road bridge near Linton.
57 Wetherby [SE 404480]. Access/egress is on the left in the park, launching left

or right above the weir and relaunching under the road bridge. The weir may not be shootable in some water conditions.

58½ Flint Mill Grange Weir. This weir is dangerous and must be inspected. Shoot or portage on the right hand side.

60 Thorp Arch [SE 431459]. At low to normal water levels this weir has loose blocks right across the base, where a large stopper forms at high water levels. The weir can be shot on the left hand side or portaged on the right bank.

63 Easedike. There is a public footpath on the left bank.

63½ Newton Kyme. There is a public footpath on the right bank.

64½ Shaws Farm. There is a public footpath on the right bank.

65½ Tadcaster [SE 488435]. Access/egress is possible on the right bank before the bridge. Shoot the weir on the left. The river is now tidal.

67¾ Kirkby Wharf. There is a public footpath on the right bank.

68¾ Ulleskelf. There is a public footpath on the right bank.

69½ Ozendyke. The road adjoins the river along this stretch. There are steep muddy banks and dense undergrowth.

71 Ryther. The road adjoins the river, again with steep muddy banks and dense undergrowth.

74¼ Wharfe's Mouth. Here the river enters the River Ouse.

75 Cawood [SE 575379]. Egress is possible near the Toll Bridge.

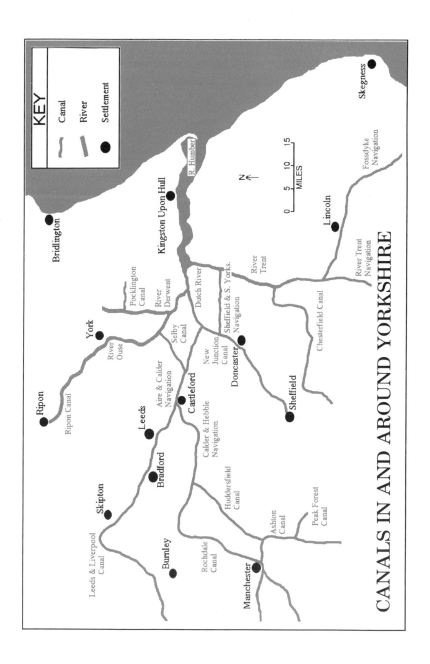

CANALS IN AND AROUND YORKSHIRE

KEY

⌇ Canal

│ River

● Settlement

R. Humber

Bridlington

Kingston Upon Hull

Skegness

Pocklington Canal

River Derwent

York

Ripon

Ripon Canal

River Ouse

Selby Canal

Dutch River

Aire & Calder Navigation

Castleford

New Junction Canal

Sheffield & S. Yorks. Navigation

Doncaster

River Trent

Leeds

Calder & Hebble Navigation

Bradford

Huddersfield Canal

Sheffield

Chesterfield Canal

River Trent Navigation

Lincoln

Fossdyke Navigation

Skipton

Leeds & Liverpool Canal

Burnley

Rochdale Canal

Ashton Canal

Peak Forest Canal

Manchester

N

MILES

0   5   10   15

NAVIGATIONS AND CANALS

There is an extensive network of inland waterways in and around Yorkshire, many of which are owned or controlled by the British Waterways Board (BWB). Consisting mainly of man-made canals and a few navigable rivers, most of them are available for canoeing.

Canoeists must have a valid licence to paddle BWB waterways. Individual membership of the BCU includes a licence to use these waterways and no further payment is required. Further licences are available to clubs for use by members. Each canoe should, however, display a current BCU Access Sticker with the Membership Number clearly visible. Otherwise users require a 'Pleasure Boat Licence' and this is available for various durations from 1 day up to 12 months.

The BWB also requires that paddlers wear suitable buoyancy aids and that all groups are accompanied by experienced leaders. Portage should be used around locks to conserve water stocks. Local advice, information, application forms and scales of charges can be obtained from the Area Leisure Officer at:

British Waterways Board
Lock Lane
CASTLEFORD WF10 2LH
(Tel 0977 554351)

Canoeists are subject to the BWB licensing conditions and bye-laws. Care should be taken when canoeing tunnels; some are prohibited to canoes whilst others may be used subject to safety precautions. Gaining access for canoeing on the following commercial waterways requires special permission from the BWB: Aire and Calder Navigation, New Junction Canal and the Sheffield and South Yorkshire Navigation (between Bramwith Lock and Rotherham Lock).

Other navigation authorities in the region include:

Associated British Ports (River Ouse - Trent Falls to Goole)
Ouse and Foss Navigation Trust (River Ouse - Goole to Waddington Ings)
Linton Lock Commissioners (River Ouse - Waddington Ings to Swale Nab)
Rochdale Canal Company (Rochdale Canal).